Christian Fashion 101

Christian FashioN 101

WHY YOU DRESS THE WAY YOU DO

AMARACHI OCHE

GRACEWORKS PUBLISHERS

CHRISTIAN FASHION 101

Author's Contact
amiephoebe@gmail.com
Tel: +234 706 4900 505

Book and Cover Design by A-graphics

Printed in the United States of America

Dedication

To all the Christian Fashion Designers

What great jobs you all are doing!

With Gratitude

To God the Father, Son and Holy Spirit I say thank You for showing me the way of life. Your love, wisdom, inspiration and guidance are incontestable.

To my husband: Oche Jonkings, and children: Excel, Shine and Reign, you rock my world in a special way. Thanks for your relentless show of love and support.

Special thanks to my loving parents Engr. & Mrs. U.U. Agomo for laying a good foundation for an honorable life. Thanks mum for those special, decent clothing styles. It has paid off.

To my brothers Chukwuma, Okem, and Chidi for your strong and affectionate brotherhood.

To my spiritual parents Dr. Pastor Paul and Dr. Mrs. Becky Enenche for quality spiritual parenting—I am watching, learning and note-taking. To my pastors, Pastor & Mrs. Oloche King Adaji and Pastor & Mrs. Ezekiel Pius, what wonderful examples you have been to me.

To Pastor Chuks Eti and Pastor Christy Ezenwokoma for your meaningful contributions toward the making of this book.

To the Convener, Damsel Arise Ministry, Mrs. Oluwaseun Okuneye for your passion to raise godly fashionistas. The story behind the writing of this book cannot be told without you.

Endorsement

This **book is not** just a fashion refinery; it is a house of purity, life, beauty, strength, light, love and sincerity. This is a powerful book that will move you from mere understanding of fashion to understanding of purpose for clothing, rediscovery of personality, and lots more.

This is a book that will refire you. The words here are not mere words. They were aesthetically written for you. They are homely, quoted and minced with so much grace.

Carefully study this book and you will understand better why you dress the way you dress. The words in here will showcase God's intent for clothing to you. As you read it, the words will be gently blown into your heart by the Refiner Himself, so you don't forget them!

This is a beautiful book everyone must read. Are you a seamstress, a fashion designer, a tailor, a dresser/fashion consultant? It's for you! Apparently, everybody can read it, as long as you wear clothes and you have passion for fashion.

By the time you are done reading this book, you would have been refined and thoroughly edified. Your fashion sense would have been re-awakened unto the honour of God, your Maker. You will love to impact your world through what you've known through this book. You will love to do the right things as touching clothing. You will love Abba the more and by the reason of your love for Him, you will get up on your feet to cause a change in the fashion world! All for God!

Oluwaseun Okuneye, Mrs.

Convener, Damsel Arise Ministry

Endorsement

There's a common phrase** that says, "The way you dress is the way you are addressed." As a child of God and also an ambassador of Jesus Christ, there is a fashion sense you ought to possess and express in and out of season. It is no news that the current fashion trend in our world today has gone bizarre and surprisingly, this trend is gradually creeping into the Church.

CHRISTIAN FASHION 101 is a masterpiece, a must-have and must-read for every Christian lady who values her body (the temple of God) and knows her worth. This mind-blowing material in your hands captures Biblical principles that can influence your fashion style assuredly.

The author has done justice to the subject matter; excellently taken time to explain why and how we can appear godly yet gorgeous with Scriptural references.

I am super excited that this book will spark a revolution in the fashion world. Enjoy and be blessed by this gift to us for such a time as this from God's own handmaiden, Mrs. Amarachi Oche-Jonkings. God bless you.

Pastor Mrs. Christy Ezenwokoma

CEO, Cking Designs Enterprise
President, Christy King Ministries

Foreword

*T*he subject of indecent dressing has sparked off a lot of controversies in our society today, especially amongst Christians. Some are angered by it; others condone it, whilst there are some who feel it is everyone's right to dress the way they deem fit no matter whose ox is gored.

In most cases, people avoid talking about it because they don't want to judge or offend others or because they feel it concerns only the youth but the reality of our times reveal it's a social malady that goes against anything and everything that is good. More worrisome is the fact that indecent dressing has become normal, even amongst believers of the Christian Faith.

In this book, the author, Mrs. Amarachi Oche-Jonkings, through the inspiration of the Holy Spirit, captures in-depth and grey areas about dressing properly and decently. The fact that some persons do not even realize that what they are wearing is offensive and misleading, makes a book like this very apt for the times we live in.

In this book, she takes us back to the beginning, as well as the significance of clothing. One of my favourite quotes in this book says: "A godly dressing starts from the intention. Why do you want to dress the way you want to? If you can strike out attraction (seduction); to feel among (trending), then you just might be set for dressing godly."

I have known the author and her family to be committed Christians. She is a motivator that is driven by her love for Christ and His Kingdom. There's no doubt that she is a practitioner of what she preaches and this book is solely for the purpose of edification and transformation.

Get set for an amazing and insightful time as you read through because you will certainly be blessed.

Don't also forget to share this book with others because it is going to change the lives of many.

Beckie Pius, Mrs.

Resident Pastor's Wife
Dunamis International Gospel Centre,
Makurdi Central, Benue State, Nigeria.

Contents

Introduction

I ***presume you are*** holding this book right in your hands because you are a Christian or an intending one, and/or you were captured by the book's title, design or summary. Whichever be your reason for wanting to get a feel its content, just know it is divinely orchestrated. Congratulations!

As you read through the pages of this book, picture yourself like you are literally taking a burden off my chest... or a yoke, my neck.

I am particularly concerned about the gradual acceptance and normalization of sensuality and nudity in the dressings of professing 'Christians'. Bodily morality seems to be dwindling with the wrap-up of the world. However, I realize that a lot of persons aren't aware of the wrongness of their clothing styles. This is one of the strong reasons this book was put together.

Have you ever seen someone wearing a particular style of clothing and you had to wonder if the person had a good look at the mirror before stepping out? You felt the person appeared like a joke in the clothes due to misfit and mismatch. I have found myself in that space. This matter is on the front burner of this book too.

The content of this book is an elaborate version of an online session I had with the members of Damsel Arise Ministry. It was such an awesome time. The revelations poured in as I typed—

many thanks to the Holy Spirit. I wanted collating some of the points and sharing as an article on social media like I usually do, but I heard to make it into a book.

Here are some participants' comments at the end of the meeting. It made my day!

- ↔ *"I want to really thank you ma for your words. My eyes have been opened, some of my dressings I didn't even know they were bad until now."*
- ↔ *"Dressing has been what the Spirit of God has been calling my attention to lately. I really loved dressing like a Tomboy but I am being cautioned by the Spirit of God and when I saw your group I was prompted to join. The lecture, wow it was indeed! The definition was so on point. The words were timely and all. Thank you ma."*

Both males and females can find this book relevant. For the most part where anything pertaining to clothing/dressing such as propriety, decency, and moderation was talked about in the Scriptures, it appeared the women were the ones being addressed more. You will find out why in this book. Men rarely had/have issues as regards these things, even though in recent times, the pants/trousers seem to be getting tighter by the day!

I implore you to read in-between the lines. Look beyond the letter that kills, but at the Spirit that gives life.

"who also made us sufficient as ministers of the new covenant, not of the letter but of the Spirit; for the letter kills, but the Spirit gives life."

2 Corinthians 3:6

At the end of each chapter, there's a key point summary; a food for thought, and helpful prayers. There's so much contained in this book. It is my prayer that you find this material invaluable. Don't just admire the truth contained herein, walk the truth! Let's get started already!

In the beginning God created the heavens and the earth.
GENESIS 1:1

With Lady Wisdom, GOD formed Earth; with Madame Insight, He raised Heaven.
PROVERBS 3:19 (MSG)

One

In The Beginning

Fashion dates as far back as "in the beginning". One of the dictionary meanings of fashion explains it to be the make or form of anything; the style, shape, appearance or mode of structure; pattern, model. It is then safe to say that the entire world is one big fashion piece created by the Master Fashion Designer- God!

Everything created by God is fashionable— the sun; the moon; the trees and flowers; the birds; the sky; the streams, rivers and ocean; and so on— each having its unique design, form and appearance. **Man was His haute couture, His masterpiece of artistry! Nothing was as stylish or exclusive as man.** He was designed-to-fit, patterned in perfection, detailed in construction, fabricated with finesse and embellished with glory.

I am certain you must have been told also, while growing up, that God made the whole world out of nothing. I had grown with that same knowledge until God interjected my thoughts one day and gave me a different narrative. While I can understand the submission of "creating something out of nothing", the truth is that He didn't. No, He didn't! **God created everything out of something.** Yes, out of Himself! Out of His GLORY! Out of His very ESSENCE!

"For everything, absolutely everything, above and below, visible and invisible, rank after rank, of angels- everything got started in Him and finds its purpose in Him."

Colossians 1:17 (MSG)

Therefore it suffices to say God 'gave birth' to the sun, sky, animals, trees, etc. He spoke into existence what was on His inside! No wonder He is referred to as the Lion of Judah, All-consuming fire, Lamb, Living Water, etc. All creation is but a kind and measure of His glory. Man being the chiefest of them all—of a higher kind and glory type—nailed it! Man was made in God's image; after His likeness!

♣♥♣

All Things Bright and Beautiful

Can you remember that nursery rhyme *"All things bright and beautiful"*?

All things bright and beautiful

All creatures great and small

All things wise and wonderful

The Lord God made them all

Nothing God made was an error. Nothing made was an accident. Nothing made was unwanted.

"Then God saw everything that He had made, and indeed it was very good. So the evening and the morning were the sixth day."

Genesis 1:31

Everything God made was *very good*. The only thing that wasn't good at the time (Adam without his Eve) was immediately addressed and made wonderful. He did not only make all things good, He also made them beautiful.

"He has made everything beautiful in its time."

Ecclesiastes 3:11

Human beings may have found a way of placing labels on themselves, and with their faulty yardstick they measure a person's beauty based on wrong parameters. But everyone is beautiful just the way he or she is. Why? Because we were created by a beautiful God *in whom* all things consist; *out of whom* all things were made! **YOU ARE BEAUTIFUL!**

♣♥♣
<u>The First Fashion Designers</u>

"Then the eyes of both were opened, and they knew that they were naked. And they sewed fig leaves together and made themselves loincloths."

Genesis 3:7 (ESV)

The first fashion designers were Adam and Eve; and the first fashion outfits were loincloths of fig leaves. They were made of purely hand-made stitches—no patterns, no embroideries, no trimmings, no design, no test-fitting, nothing! Not surprising, right? Yes, creativity is innate in every man; since we all are created in the image of God. If He designs, then we can. If He is creative, so are we; and we are in different ways, in different fields, and to varying degrees. Fashion designing is just one aspect of expression. There's fine arts, graphic designing, works of crafts, singing, acting, writing, poetry, speaking—just name it! Everyone has the ability of, at least, one form of expression. Hey, don't underestimate yourself!

> **Everyone has the ability of one form of expression.**

Today, a lot has improved in the world of fashion designing. There are lots of fashion designers, tailors and seamstresses doing good stuff and pulling great stunts! It keeps getting better.

IN THE BEGINNING

Key Point: You are created fashionable, beautiful and creative.

Food for thought: How have I viewed myself as being not as good as God sees me?

Prayer

Heavenly Father, thank You for Your awesome work of artistry on my very being. You created me in Your image, forgive me in any way I have viewed myself less than how You do. Help me see me through Your eyes. Make me a reflection of Your beauty, intelligence and creativity. Help me rise above the negativities and low opinions of people that may have subconsciously had a grip on my mind. I receive Your grace to plunge into the full expression of who You've made me, in Jesus' Name. Amen.

But if God so clothes the grass of the field, which is alive and green today and tomorrow is [cut and] thrown [as fuel] into the furnace, will He not much more clothe you? You of little faith!

MATTHEW 6:30 (AMP)

A crowd soon gathered around Jesus, and they saw the man who had been possessed by the legion of demons. He was sitting there fully clothed and perfectly sane, and they were all afraid.

MARK 5:15 (NLT)

Two

The Significance of Clothing

In **Genesis chapter three** verse seven, it reads that they sewed fig leaves together and made themselves coverings. It is therefore pertinent to note that the primary reason for clothing is for covering.

In the previous chapter, I mentioned that man was embellished with glory. As a fashion designer, clothings are embellished to make a cloth appear more beautiful, attractive, tasteful and graceful. In fascinator-making, the use of embellishments also serves to conceal hand-made stitches or knots created in the making process. Man lost the embellishment (glory) when he ate the forbidden fruit. He lost his beauty, dignity and gracefulness. He also lost his covering; exposing his deficiencies, flaws and inadequacies. All these were the spiritual implications of that singular action he took.

"Then the serpent said to the woman, "You will not surely die.

For God knows that in the day you eat of it your eyes will be opened and you will be like God, knowing good and evil."

So when the woman saw that the tree was good for food, that it was pleasant to the eyes, and a tree desirable to make one wise, she took of its fruit and ate. She also gave to her husband with her, and he ate.

Then the eyes of both of them were opened, and they knew that they were naked; and they sewed fig leaves together."

Genesis 3:4-7

♣♥♣

<u>The Physical Effect</u>

It dawned on them, like the breaking of a new day, that something had changed. A strange happening had occurred. An unusual feeling swept over them. Something was totally off. It really was awkward to see themselves stark naked. I am sure they questioned the reality of what their eyes were seeing. A while ago all was well and in order, then the next second, they were like chickens whose tail feathers a cold wind had blown against. I can almost imagine the shock on their faces! "Thank goodness! At least we are not dead as God said we would!" was probably what their mouths could mutter. Then, taking a second look at themselves, they concluded that they really were naked—their eyes weren't playing tricks on them after all! There and then, their instincts revealed the abnormality of their nakedness (as should still be today).

"And they heard the sound of the LORD God walking in the garden in the cool of the day, and Adam and his wife hid themselves from the presence of the LORD God among the trees of the garden.

Then the LORD God called to Adam and said to him, "Where are you?"

So he said, "I heard Your voice in the garden, and I was afraid because I was naked; and I hid myself."

Genesis 3:8-10

The above verse shows us that God hadn't seen them yet at the point when they realized their nakedness and sewed fig leaves together (verse seven). So it wasn't He who told them to do the very next thing they did which was dashing across the garden, and grappling for anything their hands could get hold of for cover. Mr. Fig saved the day!

"Their eyes were opened" means that they became able to tell right from wrong. The seed of evil was sown. Their consciences were birthed. Until then, they had no need for it. All was perfect—as perfect can be. No law. No sin. No wrong. No penalty.

> **Their consciences came alive. Until then, they had no need for it.**

♣♥♣

A More Excellent Way

How would it have been if all we had to wear were some funny-looking, short-span leaves? Not quite the expected 'wisdom' from eating one tiny, red apple! Huh…better imagined than experienced!

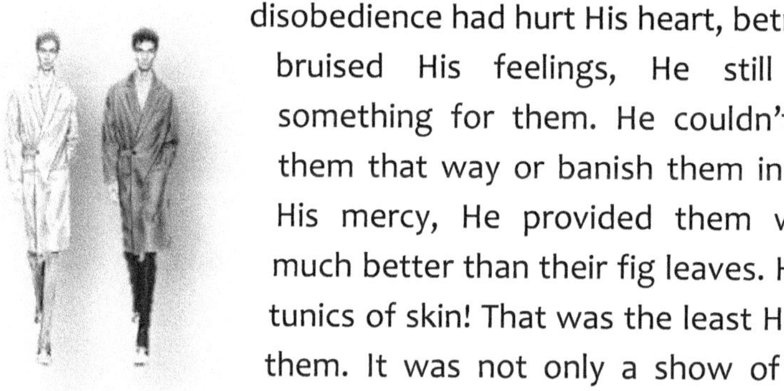

Ab initio, God has truly loved man. Even though man's disobedience had hurt His heart, betrayed His trust, bruised His feelings, He still figured out something for them. He couldn't bear to see them that way or banish them in that state. In His mercy, He provided them with clothings much better than their fig leaves. He made them tunics of skin! That was the least He could do for them. It was not only a show of achievement, superiority or instruction but also love speaking—a more excellent way!

"Also for Adam and his wife the LORD God made tunics of skin, and clothed them."

Genesis 3:21

This action of love God took towards them must have confirmed to them that they had been right in following their instincts to cover their nakedness right away. God was in support of their covering. If He wasn't maybe the writer of Genesis would have written, "And the Lord scolded Adam and Eve; saying, 'Who asked you to cover your nakedness? Are your fig leaves any better than My 'invisible clothing'? Do you know what it cost me to drape you in that? Take off those flimsy leaves and be thou 'naked' forever!'" But that wasn't the narrative in the account of man's fall. God was fully in support. In Nigeria, we would say "God supported their *fashion ministry*." He definitely had to.

♣♥♣

<u>Fig Leaves versus Tunic</u>

What is a tunic?

I had to look up the meaning of tunic. A tunic is a garment worn over the torso/trunk of the body, with or without sleeves, belted at the waist, and of various lengths ranging from the hips to the ankles. Another definition has it to be a piece of clothing that *fits loosely* over a person's body, reaching to the waist or knees and often has no sleeves. These definitions fit what we see the Israelites wear in historic Bible movies.

As much as I want to applaud Adam and Eve's ingenuity, their fig leaves weren't good enough. They were limiting and less dignifying. Perhaps God was trying to pass a message across to them with the tunic, that they needed something more decent, more covering, more honorable, more comfortable, and more durable. Only after His provision of the tunic did He feel satisfied enough to evict them from the Garden they called home.

The tunic served as a model. For all the times I've had to see graphic representations of the story of Adam and Eve, they showed them with fig leaves covering their private parts, that is, Eve's genital and her breasts; and for Adam, his genitals alone. Obviously, in comparison with the tunic, God wasn't comfortable with this. Certain areas of their bodies

> **The tunic served as a model.**

still needed to be properly covered.

See The Message version of Genesis 3:7

"Immediately the two of them did see what was really going on—saw themselves naked! They sewed fig leaves together as MAKESHIFT clothes for themselves."

Genesis 3:7 (MSG)

Their fig leaves clothes were makeshifts! A makeshift is something that is a temporary (usually insubstantial) substitution. It seems to me as though some persons still go out today in makeshift clothes like there's a plan to substitute it with something better they took along in their bags. The fig leaves lacked substance while the tunic had substance. The Message version calls the tunic, 'leather clothing'. Solid! The fig leaves were of plant origin, the tunic of animal origin. You remember the Nigerian "khaki no be leather" idiom? This is where it applies (smiles). The fig leaves and the tunic were not mates at all ("Khaki no be leather", that is, "khaki is not leather" is said when trying to show the superiority of something over another). The fig leaves were no match for the tunic at all.

If I could read God's mind at the time He was making the tunic/leather clothing, perhaps He must have thought to Himself, "No way am I going to let the man and his woman debase themselves in this manner. Do they think they are comparable to any other creature I made? Even though no clothes they would ever make to wear can match the natural one they lost (*"So why do you worry about clothing? Consider the lilies of the field, how they grow: they neither toil nor spin;*

and yet I say to you that even Solomon in all his glory was not arrayed like one of these." Matthew 6:28-29), they still need to make good whatever dignity they have left."

Let's zoom in a little on the word 'insubstantial'. For their fig leaves to have been insubstantial, it also meant that it was inappropriate to suit the purpose for which it was worn. Their fig leaves might have been good in the garden but definitely not outside the garden. Some clothes are best worn only in the presence of one's spouse, within the confines of one's room and not for public viewership. Knowing the difference requires the fear of God.

In another vein, it is inappropriate or improper to dress formal when you should be informal and vice-versa. There are corporate, casual and traditional wears. Some persons have lost out on job opportunities, contract, marriages and favors based on their wrong appearances. You don't dress to an interview like you are going for a party. Who does that? Another inappropriate thing people do is to wear a flowery-patterned top on a differently patterned skirt/trouser. Only gardens are permitted to appear like that. It is also wrong fashion-wise to wear stripes on stripes or stripes on flowered. What is preferable is either you go plain on top and striped/flowery below or vice-versa. Wearers' discretion is strongly advised (laughs).

THE SIGNIFICANCE OF CLOTHING

Key Point: Being naked or half-naked, because of man's fall, is abnormal.

Food for thought: In what ways do I appear in makeshift clothes?

Prayer

Dear God, thank You for loving me with an everlasting love. Your timely provisions are second to none. While we were 'naked', we were covered with Your glory, love and warmth. Even so now, that clothing has become an important basic need of man, You've made it a point of duty to take the worry off me, ensuring I am provided for— for I am of more value than the lilies of the field You clothe. Today, I ask for the grace to partner with You to appear dignifying and honorable in the clothes I wear, in Jesus' Name. Amen.

So rejoice, O Heavens, and all who live there, but doom to earth and sea, for the devil's come down on you with both feet; he's had a great fall; he's wild and raging with anger; he hasn't much time and he knows it.

REVELATIONS 12:12 (MSG)

The serpent was the shrewdest of all the wild animals the LORD God had made. One day he asked the woman, "Did God really say you must not eat the fruit from any of the trees in the garden?"

GENESIS 3:1 (NLT)

Three

The Contradiction

We *have established that* one importance of clothing is covering. However, let's retrospect a bit to understand the necessity of clothing. Why was it necessary for them to put on coverings? **With the fall of man, the freedom to move about naked was lost.** That was a reality that had turned to a mere wish. As far as being on earth is concerned, that was an opportunity they could never again rightly have. Clothes became a necessary part of man, stamped and approved by God; with His tunic as a model/guide to what man would create thereafter. Let's wade deeper.

Of course, they had no reason whatsoever to feel any shame. Not only because they were draped in God's glory, but also for their minds which had not been corrupted with sin (the knowledge of evil). They didn't and couldn't even recognize 'nakedness'. When they looked at each other, all they saw in the other was the covering of glory, beauty and love. In that state, they didn't know what evil was, what lust was. Adam looked at his woman and saw a beautiful variant of his handsome self. He saw perfection (a perfectly sculpted personality God had brought him, resembling nothing but himself...just with slight physical variations—a different version). There were no negative feelings buzzing from him toward her. No desire of lust. No imagination/nursed-thought of someone else with a different vibe, shade, shape or features—other than Eve his wife—ran through his mind. She was all he knew and was satisfied with all of her attributes; and vice-versa. Everything was just fine between them until…

> **Their minds had not yet been corrupted with sin. Adam thought of/desired no other.**

♣♥♣

Who Came Knocking?

Since his name changed from Lucifer to Satan, everything in him resonated with evil—Devil (Desperately evil). The Book of John, chapter ten verse ten says that the thief comes to steal, kill and destroy. The thief here is the devil. He is not as inventive as people think him to be. In fact, he lost with his fall, creativity and ingenuity. He only knows to steal, twist and turn God's original and existing designs, patterns and formulae to birth his own substandard ideas. He is anti-God. He seeks to destroy God's plan, will and intention. God willed that man be properly covered and clothed but the devil wills otherwise, knowing that lust—**a foremost precursor of sin**—has been built with man's fall.

On the flip side, he also wants to ensure man is in shame. Little wonder why **people afflicted by the demon of insanity lose every form of dignity and self-esteem in how they look**—clad with tattered, humiliating and offensive clothes. It reveals the nature of the kind of spirit responsible for insanity—the real nature of Satan —ugly, shamed, dishonored, empty and dark personality. People who are *deliberately* nude and seductive are no different from the mad person. They only are on the other end of the spectrum! To be fully clothed is to be perfectly sane (*Mark 5:15*).

It's a great delight to the devil to see man short of or less than what God desires for him. Anything that thwarts God's original intention, count the devil in. What a counterfeiter! What a destroyer!

"But He turned and said to Peter, "Get behind Me, Satan! You are an offense to Me, for you are not mindful of the things of God, but the things of men."

Matthew 16:23

Satan isn't mindful of the things of God but of man. He knows he stands no chance at striving with God but with man. He was able to get man; for he realized that getting man—manipulating him to go contrary to God's commandment—would hurt God invariably. This makes Satan more interested in the affairs of man. Whenever he presents an apple to you, don't be blinded by its niceness. You think he likes you? Beneath the skin of the apple are thorns. No matter how 'nice and comforting' his suggestions are, or how giddy it makes you feel, he doesn't exactly like to see you *really* happy.

> **The devil stands no chance at striving with God but man.**

The devil has counterfeits for everything. Just as some songs are inspired by him, some clothing designs are too. His old strategy of deception is still in place today. Some are deceived into believing that trendy fashion outfits, which expose a *little bit* of their cleavages, breasts and other sensitive body parts, are not *exactly overboard*. They live in this denial because Satan has a doctorate degree in 'wrongrightology' (study of making what is wrong look right). That didn't start today. He has a library of journals to his credit!

"And no wonder! For Satan himself transforms himself into an angel of light.

Therefore it is no great thing if his ministers also transform themselves into ministers of righteousness, whose end will be according to their works."

2Corinthians 11:14

It is a popular saying, "We are saved by grace. Grace covers it all. It is the heart that matters." Oh! If only you understand what grace is!

There really isn't any point showing what God wants covered. We've left the Garden of Eden!

♣♥♣

The Crafty Harlot

I had once lived in an area where there was a brothel. It was situated along a street I couldn't help but pass either to and fro Church or when running errands. On my return from Church services in the evening, I saw prostitutes already stationed outside the building, standing on the streets strategically displaying and marketing their 'goods'. As I recall their appearances right now, everything about their dressing was aimed at revealing their SELLING POINTS; from their breasts to their stomach, to their laps and buttocks! The very things God covered in the beginning! I am reminded of this scriptural passage.

> **Everything about a harlot's dressing reveals her selling points.**

"For at the window of my house I looked through my lattice,

And saw among the simple, I perceived among the youths, a young man devoid of understanding,

Passing along the street near her corner; and he took the path to her house

In the twilight, in the evening, in the black and dark night.

And there a woman met him, with the attire of a harlot, and a crafty heart.

She was loud and rebellious, her feet would not stay at home.

At times she was outside, at times in the open square, lurking at every corner.

So she caught him and kissed him; with an impudent face she said to him:

I have peace offerings with me; today I have paid my vows.

So I came out to meet you, diligently to seek your face, and I have found you.

I have spread my bed with tapestry, colored coverings of Egyptian linen.

I have perfumed my bed with myrrh, aloes, and cinnamon.

Come, let us take our fill of love until morning; let us delight ourselves with love.

For my husband is not at home; he has gone on a long journey;

He has taken a bag of money with him, and will come home on the appointed day."

With her enticing speech she caused him to yield, with her flattering lips she seduced him.

Immediately he went after her, as an ox goes to the slaughter or as a fool to the correction of the stocks,

Till an arrow struck his liver. As a bird hastens to the snare, he did not know it would cost his life.

Now therefore, listen to me, my children; pay attention to the words of my mouth:

Do not let your heart turn aside to her ways, do not stray into her paths;

For she has cast down many wounded, and all who were slain by her were strong men.

Her house is the way to hell, descending to the chambers of death."

Proverbs 7:6-27

This is a whole lot of scriptures but not with few points to extrapolate.

- ❖ Verse 10 says "and there was a woman with the attire of a harlot." There is an ATTIRE/a DRESSING/a CLOTHING of a harlot. Period! There is a look of a harlot. There are certain outfits that can classify one as a harlot. There is an appearance associated with harlotry. **Beyond the actual job description, the look is enough for the nomenclature.**
- ❖ The woman in this narration was not a harlot. She was the wife of a man who had gone on a long journey. She only *played the harlot.* This substantiates the point above.
- ❖ She appeared in a harlot's attire for a reason and for a season. She must have understudied a harlot and understood her game: sensuality; consistent and persistent public show; seduction; and enticement. *See Verse 12.* What a crafty harlot!
- ❖ A harlot's game is never a goalless one. There's always an end in view which is to physically lure to bed but spiritually wound, slay, destroy, ruin and kill destinies.

> **A harlot's game is never a goalless one.**

❖ A harlot never works alone. Verse 27 says her house is the way to hell, descending to the chambers of death. Whose business is hell? You already know. She clearly is on the devil's mission either knowingly or unknowingly. She's got the backing of her employer (Satan), recruiting people to his organization (hell); utilizing his strategies of the lust of the eyes, lust of the flesh (verses 10-18) and pride of life (verses 19-21). Yes, pride of life! Don't be surprised that the mention of her husband's unavailability to the man in the story may have opened a window for a contest in his mind, leading him to embark on an ego trip. Perhaps he thought he might be better off in bed than her husband (something he would take pride in). The spirit of conquest is in the heart of every man.

There is an attire of a harlot; whether you support the attribution or not. Yes, you may not be a prostitute, like the woman in the story; and if you aren't, what's the motive behind appearing like one? What business do you have with her *kind of clothes*? Why consider acting her role, and sending the wrong signals about who you are not?

Satan knows he has but a short time.

Tick tock, says the clock

Down to abyss, he won't miss

Souls to confine, he's signed to find

Like a scorcher to torture

Forever and ever

His mission for each new day is to cause as many to fall or draw back unto perdition.

There are many means to this end. One of which is sexual immorality (masturbation, bestiality, homosexuality, adultery and fornication) sponsored by pornography and indecency.

Let's round off this chapter with the following Scriptural passage, as it ushers us into the next.

"Just because something is technically legal doesn't mean it is spiritually appropriate. If I went around doing whatever I thought I could get by with, I'd be a slave to many whims.

You know the old saying, "First you eat to live, and then you live to eat?" Well, it may be true that the body is only a temporary thing, but that's no excuse for stuffing your body with food, or indulging it with sex. Since the Master honors you with a body, honor Him with your body!

God honored the Master's body by raising it from the grave. He'll treat yours with the same resurrection power.

Until that time, remember that your bodies are created with the same dignity as the Master's body. You wouldn't take the Master's body off to a whorehouse, would you? I should hope not.

There's more to sex than mere skin on skin. **Sex is as much spiritual mystery as physical fact.** As written in Scripture, "The two become one."

Since we want to become spiritually one with the Master, we must not pursue the kind of sex that avoids commitment and intimacy, leaving us more lonely than ever—the kind of sex that can never "become one."

There is a sense in which sexual sins are different from all others. In sexual sin we violate the sacredness of our own bodies, these bodies that were made for God-given and God-modeled love, for "becoming one" with another.

Or didn't you realize that our body is a sacred place, the place of the Holy Spirit? Don't you see that you can't live however you please; squandering what God paid such a high price for? The physical part of you is not some piece of property belonging to the spiritual part of you.

God owns the whole works. So let people see God in and through your body."

1 Corinthians 6:12-20 (MSG)

THE CONTRADICTION

Key Point: The devil sponsors rebellion, disobedience, nudity, fornication, adultery and shame.

Food for thought: Have I at any time collaborated or cooperated with the devil in my dressing? What can I improve on going forward?

Prayer

Heavenly Father, Merciful You are. I see my wrong, and I ask that Your mercy gives me a clean sheet of record. I can clearly see the devil for who he really is now. I ask that every lie I have believed, that has informed and formed my poor choices of clothing styles, be torn down. If ever I have aided and abetted the act of sexual immorality knowingly or unknowingly, forgive me. I receive Your grace to appear in such a way that people see You in and through my body, in Jesus' Name. Amen.

Now Tamar was wearing a [long-sleeved] robe of various colors; for that is how the virgin daughters of the kings dressed themselves in robes.

2 SAMUEL 13:18 (AMP)

Don't be concerned about the outward beauty of fancy hairstyles, expensive jewelry, or beautiful clothes. You should clothe yourselves instead with the beauty that comes from within, the unfading beauty of a gentle and quiet spirit, which is so precious to God.

1 PETER 3:3-4 (NLT)

Four

The Christian and Fashion

Fashion means so many different things to different people. Should a Christian be fashionable? Does our dressing reflect who we are or aren't? What is the yardstick for measuring decency? These and more are the questions this chapter would address. But first, who does the "Christian" in the chapter's topic refer to? We need to know this Christian to be able to appreciate his/her involvement in the world of fashion.

♣♥♣

<u>Who Is A Christian?</u>

The first place the word 'Christian' was mentioned was in Acts 11:26. The word is translated Christ-like, that is, having a semblance of Jesus the Christ. One doesn't automatically become Christ-like in nature (conduct and conversation). Being Christ-like is a product of fellowship, dedication and time. No baby becomes an adult on the self-same day of birth. So it is with spiritual birth.

The Book of Acts chapter four gives an account of Peter and John who had been apprehended for healing a lame man and preaching in Jesus' Name. As they stood before the court to defend themselves, the Holy Spirit empowered Peter's speech causing him to boldly respond with utterances he ordinarily couldn't have put together. What struck the court's panel was the fact that they were ordinary fishermen who were unschooled and untrained! How on earth were they able to articulate their points?! The only thing that doused their marvel was when they realized that **THEY HAD BEEN WITH JESUS!** Indeed, association brings about assimilation.

> **Being Christ-like isn't automatic.**

"Now when they saw the boldness of Peter and John, and perceived that they were uneducated and untrained men, they marveled. And they realized that they had been with Jesus."

Acts 4:13

That being said, here are some points on who a Christian is.

- ✓ A Christian is a believer. A person who believes in the Trinity (God the Father, Son and Holy Spirit). Consequently, he/she believes in the death and resurrection of Jesus as the only way to the Father.

- ✓ A Christian is someone who seeks to live his or her life according to the principles and values taught by Jesus

Christ. I particularly like this definition because it helps differentiate a churchgoer from a Christian. Read the definition again. Take a breather and let it sink in... Okay, welcome back.

"...living life according to the principles and values taught by Jesus Christ."

Jesus taught a million and one things in His brief stay on earth. He did physically (through His sermons and parables—the Gospels) and also spiritually (by His Spirit, through God-breathed scriptures—the Epistles). He didn't fail to establish one thing, and that is the Kingdom of Heaven—its tenets and our responsibilities toward it. He talked of us being the light of the world; the salt of the earth. We are to set the standards and pace. **We are to illuminate the darkness around us, not dim our lights or hide it under a bushel and play safe.**

"You are the salt of the earth; but if the salt loses its flavor, how shall it be seasoned?

It is then good for nothing but to be thrown out and trampled underfoot by men.

You are the light of the world. A city that is set on a hill cannot be hidden.

Nor do they light a lamp and put it under a basket, but on a lampstand, and it gives light to all who are in the house.

Let your light so shine before men, that they may see your good works and glorify your Father in heaven."

Matthew 5:13-16

In the epistles, Apostle Paul calls a Christian a new creation and an ambassador.

A Christian has the responsibilities of being an ambassador of God's Kingdom.

"Therefore, if anyone is in Christ, he is a new creation; old things have passed away; behold, all things have become new.

Now then, we are ambassadors for Christ, as though God were pleading through us: we implore you on Christ's behalf, be reconciled to God."

2 Corinthians 5:17, 20

✓ A Christian is one who was once imperfect but has believed in and received a perfect Christ, duly represented by His Spirit- the Holy Spirit, and yields to the guidance of the Spirit.

"For as many as are led by the Spirit of God, these are sons of God."

Romans 8:14

✓ A Christian is one who consciously walks the path of perfection, righteousness and holiness, relying on the grace of God while at it.

"Be ye therefore perfect, even as your Father who is in heaven is perfect."

Matthew 5:48 (KJV)

"Therefore, having these promises, beloved, let us cleanse ourselves from all filthiness of the flesh and spirit, perfecting holiness in the fear of God."

2 Corinthians 7:1

"But now having been set free from sin, and having become slaves of God, you have your fruit to holiness, and the end, everlasting life."

Romans 6:22

"If indeed you have heard Him and have been taught by Him, as the truth is in Jesus:

that you put off, concerning your former conduct, the old man which grows corrupt according to the deceitful lusts,

and be renewed in the spirit of your mind,

and that you put on the new man which was created according to God, in true righteous and holiness."

Ephesians 4:21-24

"For God did not call us to uncleanness, but in holiness."

1 Thessalonians 4:7

"Pursue peace with all people, and holiness, without which no one will see the Lord."

Hebrews 12:14

✓ A Christian is a lover; one who loves God enough to bring Him pleasure by doing His commandments.

"If you love Me, keep My commandments"

John 14:15

"My little children, let us not love in word or in tongue, but in deed and in truth.

And by this we know that we are of the truth, and shall assure our hearts before Him.

For if our heart condemns us, God is greater than our heart, and knows all things

Beloved, if our heart does not condemn us, we have confidence toward God.

And whatever we ask we receive from Him, because we keep His commandments and do those things that are pleasing in His sight.

And this is His commandment: that we should believe on the name of His Son Jesus Christ and love one another, as He gave us commandment."

1 John 3:18-23

"For this is the love of God, that we keep His commandments. And His commandments are not burdensome."

1 John 5:3

In loving one another, a Christian is mindful of his actions as it affects others who are in the world with him. Yes, it's 'your life' but it isn't ALWAYS about you. Besides, this 'your life' really isn't yours! It no longer belongs to you. It has been bought with a high price.

"Don't you realize that your body is the temple of the Holy Spirit, who lives in you and was given to you by

God? You do not belong to yourself, for God bought you with a high price."

1 Corinthians 6:19 (NLT)

Now, considering others in your actions could mean avoiding certain things, not because they are 'wrong' in themselves but for the sake of another who is 'weak'.

"But beware lest somehow this liberty of yours become a stumbling block to those who are weak."

1 Corinthians 8:13

The reason for this point is this: I have heard 'Christians' say that Christianity is a heart thing; trying to say that it's more of the spiritual than the physical. It's more of the inward than the outward. They can dress the way they like, in what makes them feel good and happy about themselves, even if it is erotic. Their spirituality shouldn't be judged based on what they wear or how they appear but based on their attitudinal disposition. Okay, fine. No doubt! Yes, it's a heart thing; but only God knows a man by his heart.

> **Christianity is both inward and outward.**

"And He said to them, "You are those who justify yourselves before men, but God knows your hearts. For what is highly esteemed among men is an abomination in the sight of God."

Luke 16:15

We—humans—know by the fruits; fruits unto godliness!

"You will know them by their fruits. Do men gather grapes from thornbushes or figs from thistles?"

Matthew 7:16

The totality of a Christian is important. The spirit, soul and body must be blameless.

"Now may the God of peace Himself sanctify you completely; and may your whole **spirit, soul, and body be preserved blameless** at the coming of our Lord Jesus Christ."

1 Thessalonians 5:23

In Romans 14:14-23, food was the bone of contention. There were certain foods God forbade the Jews from eating. The coming of Jesus, and His free-for-all salvation package, gave rise to non-Jewish Christians. There was a mix of believers (Jews and Greeks). The Greeks were not subjected to the Jewish laws on what and what not to eat. This created controversies within the Christian community at the time. Some Jews were offended at the Greeks who didn't follow that law and also at their fellow Jews who behaved like the Greeks in not keeping the law. In Paul's wisdom and by the Spirit, this was what he had to say:

"I know and am convinced by the Lord Jesus that there is nothing unclean of itself; but to him who considers anything to be unclean, to him it is unclean.

Yet if your brother is grieved because of your food, you are no longer walking in love. Do not destroy with your food the one for whom Christ died.

Therefore do not let your good be spoken of as evil;

For the kingdom of God are not eating and drinking, but righteousness and peace and joy in the Holy Spirit.

For he who serves Christ in these things is acceptable to God and approved by men.

Therefore let us pursue the things which make for peace and the things by which one may edify another.

Do not destroy the work of God for the sake of food. All things indeed are pure, but it is evil for the man who eats with offense.

It is good neither to eat meat nor drink wine nor do anything by which your brother stumbles or is offended or is made weak
Do you have faith? Have it to yourself before God. Happy is he who does not condemn himself in what he approves.

But he who doubts is condemned if he eats, because he does not eat from faith; for whatever is not from faith is sin."

Romans 14:14-23

For the purpose of this book, perhaps we could replace food with our clothing style. How does that pass for a substitute? Suitable, right? So, bearing in mind the consequences of some of our choices and actions on others is a sign of love. Am I saying you should walk on egg shells because of others? Not really. Love is conscious; conscious of the fact that there exist in the world, others apart from you.

Love isn't love on its own. It loses its name, nature and existence when there is no other party involved— the very reason God formed man; so that His Nature of love can be expressed. Love has meaning *only* when there's an object of affection.

> *Love is kind and thoughtful. It is not proud or arrogant. It is not self-seeking. It doesn't rejoice at injustice but rejoices with the truth [when right and truth prevail]. Love believes all things [looking for the best in each one].*

Excerpts from 1 Corinthians 13:4-7 (AMP)

> **Love fails to exist without an object of affection.**

Let me first state here that nothing justifies a rapist's action; the same goes for every other sin. A bad person is a bad person. Period! Exposed or covered, a rapist would go for anyone as long as that urge comes and remains untamed (especially the sexually immoral kind of rapist). A woman who displays her goods (say, food items) for sale in the market place is as much exposed to thieves as her potential customers. It would be to her detriment to go hiding her goods for fear of thieves and miss out on her potential customers (this is the reasonable argument usually presented that I buy into;

notwithstanding, it is behooveful to make it known that the sales of food items and dressing indecently do not have the same moral ranking). Be that as it may, we should bear in mind the fact that she having something a thief finds stealable makes her prone to theft; so it is with someone who dresses indecently (we will get a clearer picture shortly). However, the thief when caught would not have his excuse of hunger/poverty tenable when there are other ways he could have catered for that. **The bottom line remains: there is no right reason for wrongdoing**.

Seizing this opportunity that has presented itself, and considering the rape incidences reported in recent times around us, I would love us to look at rape with a holistic lens (the "why" it even occurs); some rape incidences stem from psychological issues like childhood abuse— ACE (Adverse Childhood Experience)—emotional baggage; revenge; and even sadistic tendencies (for the fun of it as long as pain is inflicted on another). It could even also be spiritual. I read of a true-life story of a man who raped his mother, grandmother and a myriad of others because a female classmate he raped and deflowered while in secondary school (in a bid to revenge her overthrowing him from the first position he occupied in class) placed a curse on him and his generation. The curse caught up with him and his only daughter who, at the time of recounting his experience, had been raped thrice. Lastly, we have those (the loose, immoral ones) who consume a high dose of porn with or without the influence of substances. These ones act with the slightest provocation toward that unfortunate victim based on how negatively occupied their thoughts are.

Nevertheless, for the sake of persons who aren't rapists, whose consciences are tender; fighting hard to die their dirty old habits; struggling to overcome secret sins; learning the art of self-control, you've got to do everything within your power to rule out yourself as someone's trigger! As a Christian, it is not a space you should find yourself in. Don't be an accomplice to a crime. Don't assist someone to sin. When it comes to sensuality (that is, what turns men on), most men are visual; as women are emotional. Men admit they are. Ask them or should I say ask King David? His sexual escapade with Bathsheba was rather unfortunate and avoidable (2 Samuel 11). During a Bible discussion on this chapter, some persons threw the blame at Bathsheba, others at David; well, story for another day. While the circumstance surrounding David's error may be quite different from the discourse at hand, one thing remains common—arousal by sight. **How that arousal is handled, is where grace steps in; grace imparts self-control (Titus 2:11).** I had wanted writing *"how that arousal is handled, is what differentiates the 'boys' from the 'men'; the 'babe' from the 'mature'."*

> **Men are visual, women are emotional.**

But then I realized that even the mighty can fall. We know King David to be a man after God's heart. He had a deep relationship with God. For the records, God had made a promise to him four chapters ago (2 Samuel 7), yet he fell prey to the lust of the eyes and flesh.

Sisters, help our brothers not to be guilty of the offence in Matthew 5:28. It reads, *"But I say to you that whoever looks at a woman to lust for her has already committed adultery with her in his heart."*

✓ A Christian knows that he/she is called and accountable. Nothing done is without the knowledge of our Creator.

"So then each of us shall give account of himself to God."

Romans 14:12

The above stated points of who a Christian is are noteworthy if every other thing contained in this book would add up for you. I painstakingly committed fifteen pages to spell the word C-H-R-I-S-T-I-A-N. Phew! That's a lot. I perhaps would have done more but that would mean changing the title of the book (laughs).

Christianity involves a whole lot. Little wonder Jesus said that the way that leads to eternal life is narrow. He taught hard truths–*"Therefore many of His disciples, when they heard this, said, 'This is a hard saying; who can understand it?'" John 6:60.*

He also likened the Christian walk to carrying a cross and losing one's life.

"Then Jesus said to His disciples, "If anyone desires to come after Me, let him deny himself, and take up his cross, and follow Me. For whoever desires to save his life will lose it, but whoever loses his life for My sake will find it."

Matthew 16:24-25

We are in the world but not of the world and are hated by the world.

"I have given them your word; and the world has hated them because they are not of the world, just as I am not of the world."

John 17:14

The Christian life is a call. It's a call to a new life; a call to a changed life. A change only the Holy Spirit can make inside of a person given to the teachings in the school of the Spirit; through habitual communion of reading and studying the believer's syllabus (the Bible), partaking in group discussions (praying, and fellowshipping with other believers & their literatures). It is also a faith-life because even God acted in faith and hope to have risked the death of His only Son for an uncertain bunch of sinners who could disregard and reject His offer of salvation at will. He must have had a bet on this: **that to personally live in the hearts of men was the only way out of, and the permanent solution to the unrighteousness of men.** Today, because of this, He is not afraid to ask anyone (no matter how neck-deep in sin) to come as he/she is. He's got it covered! He is so confident of the change-creating effect His Presence has. Therefore, it is like an insult on God for any man to claim to have had Christ with no evidence of a changed life, sooner or later. His grace is sufficient. His nature is contagious. God says to come as you are but not remain as you are. You can't keep being a deliberate sinner.

> **It is like an insult on God for any man to claim to have had Christ with no evidence of a changed life, sooner or later.**

"When Jesus had raised Himself up and saw no one but the woman, He said to her, "Woman, where are those accusers of yours? Has no one condemned you?"

She said, "No one, Lord." And Jesus said to her, "Neither do I condemn you; go and sin no more."

Then Jesus spoke to them again, saying, "I am the light of the world. He who follows Me shall not walk in darkness, but have the light of life."

John 8:10-12

The passage above is the story of a woman that was caught in the act of adultery (I wonder why her accomplice wasn't brought along with her. That's by the way). She was brought to Jesus to trap Him. Some expected Him to condemn her. But in His wisdom, He did what He did and said what He said (see the Bible for the full story). He neither condemned her nor did He applaud her for her act. He wasn't indifferent either. He accepted her, spoke lovingly to her, and released her to **"go and sin no more"**, for it was enough she had just encountered Him— Love, Grace and Light!

The Christian life is a sweet and honorable experience. It's a highly rewarding one too. It's a big deal to have the Creator of the entire universe live inside of you!

***If you want to become this renewed, reconnected, redeemed, restored, revived, recreated born-again Christian, please say the prayer in the Appendix 1 ***

♣♥♣
Just How Fashionable?

As a fashion designer, I love it when my creativity comes to the fore. I believe in being fashionable as long as I don't make a god out of fashion. I love wearing designs that wow people; giving them a good stare for their eyes (laughs). Wait a minute, just before you go thinking of me as carnal, it's the same way I am in awe of the beauty of nature and creation I see all around me. Many a time I've been stopped in my tracks by the mental images the sky and cloud create. Each day gives a different,

beautiful, unique design of the firmament. The natural landscapes are equally beautifully fashionable. Nature is simply wonderful. God's works are wondrous!

Consequently, by implication, you owe it as a duty to God to represent His Kingdom duly. I once had a conversation with a woman who was up and about asking for financial assistance, as she had spent a good fortune on health issues. I wouldn't bore you with the details. I offered the help I could but I didn't fail to utilize that golden opportunity to preach Christ to her and invite her to the healing and deliverance service and other church services of my place of fellowship. She blurted out how the only challenge she had with my invitation was what she had to wear! To her, my church is for 'big' people, that is, financially buoyant people. How would what she had to wear match what people who attended the church wore?! Won't she be treated commonly and given a seat amongst 'commoners'?

I could understand her concerns but quickly debunked her notions. One, no such thing existed. Two, who cared about what you wore or didn't wear? Maybe there are those who do, but I am certain there are a one hundred and one-me in there who do not ex-act-ly care! I advised her to come like God gave her an appointment to meet with Him. Finally, I didn't fail to let her realize that we are to look good and beautiful. I pointed her attention to everything natural her eyes could see, as to how painstakingly pretty God made them. She nodded in agreement. It doesn't even have to be expensive to look good. Honestly.

Per time, we should cut our coats according to our cloths with every relish of gratitude! If your current level of wears is Okrika (OK), that is, second-handed clothes, you are not in any way disadvantaged. With proper furbishing, you may end up looking like the boutique-kind. You, the wearer of the garment, are the expensive one; and by extension, your clothing is implicated. Do you remember the story of Jesus' triumphal entry into Jerusalem? Ordinarily, no one would have thrown pieces of clothing or palm leaves for a donkey. But because Jesus was on that donkey, its worth stepped up. It enjoyed the same privileges. Bro/Sis, it is in the carriage. It is in what we call 'packaging' When you have more resources at your disposal, you can decide to change your game if you so wish.

> **Understanding what fits body type**
> **+**
> **Blending colors appropriately**
> **= basic fashionability**

Being fashionable isn't exactly far-fetched. Yes, for real. Understanding your body type/shape and what fits it (not every style *may* fit you) and blending colors appropriately (because the last time I checked, rainbows appear only in the sky and they don't have two legs) are basically it.

Concerning body types, we have primarily 5 of them. These shapes are God-given or resultant alterations due to bad feeding and living habits. They are:

1. **Inverted triangle:** This means you are bigger on top. Your bust and/or shoulder measurements are fuller/wider than your hips and buttocks.
2. **Triangle (pear shape):** This is the opposite of the first. You are bigger on the bottom. Your hips are fuller than your top part.
3. **Oval (apple shape):** There's that extra in the middle of you. Maybe from excessive eating and accumulation of fat in the thoracic and abdominal regions.
4. **Hourglass:** This is a curvy person who has a defined waistline, a full bust and full hips resulting in the hourglass figure. Figure eight per se.
5. **Rectangle (banana shape):** A person with this shape has a very little difference in the measurement between her chest, waist and hip measurement.

For instance, someone with an inverted triangle shape (big bust, narrow waist, less fleshy buttocks, and narrow hips) wearing something overly hugging appears funny. Just picture it. Someone with that kind of shape would want to have dresses that give an illusion of full hips, something that balls out from the waist or so like a dress with gathers at the waist.

A flowy top, A-line dresses, flared palazzo, full/three-quarter sleeves are clothing pieces that could work just fine for such a figure. The hourglass shape is upheld by many as the *perfect* shape. So the idea is to create the illusion of that shape in what you wear, regardless of your body type.

♣♥♣

<u>Science and Art of Colours</u>

Colours are just baes! Have you ever imagined the world without them—like a black and white world? No blue sky…no red rose…no yellow sunflower…no green trees…no sea green ocean…no pink petals…no brown cats (yak! I dislike cats). Such a bore! A world without colours is better pictured in the mind! Thank God for colours and our ability to see them.

I have decided to make this a sub topic because of its import. I have heard people ask about what colours to combine with a particular fabric colour. This doesn't have to be only about clothings, the same knowledge can be applied to combining garments and other fashion accessories like jewelries, fascinators/hats/headgears, belts, bags/purses and footwear. When it comes to colour combination in fashion, it is both science and art. You either have an eye for colours or acquire knowledge on how colours interact. I will try to fill in as much details I have gathered from findings on colour mathematics and chemistry. In fashion, a colour isn't well appreciated when it stands alone; a mix of colours in a fabric sets the fabric in a proper perspective. The experts have drawn certain rules or guides in combining colours from the **colour wheel**. The colour wheel is a circular spectrum of colours invented by Sir Isaac Newton in the 18th century. It reveals the relationship of the primary, secondary and tertiary colours (just take your mind down fine-arts memory lane if you can). The colours on this wheel are basically the rainbow colours, following the same

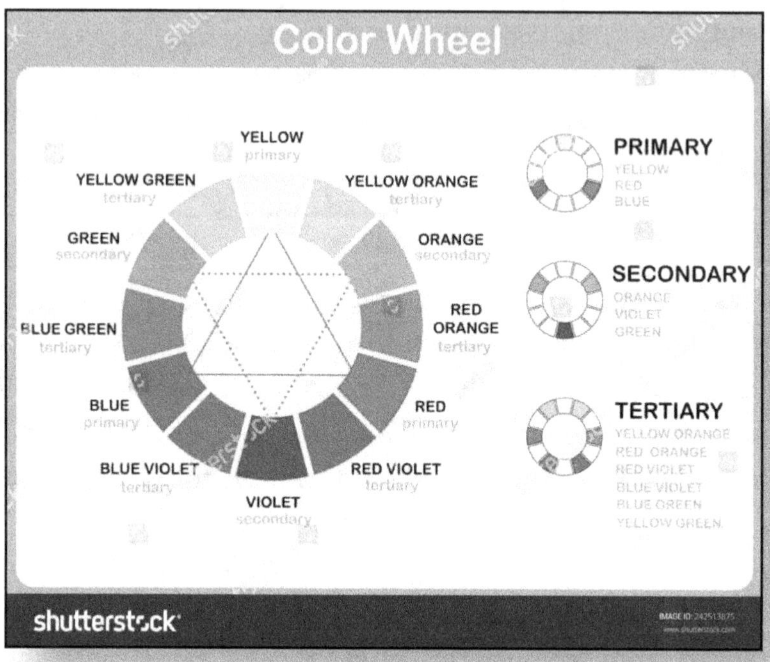

ROYGBIV sequence. Now I feel like taking it back when I wrote Isaac Newton discovered the colour wheel...I think Noah did! When colours appear good together it is referred to as **colour harmony**; Nigerians would rather say **colour blocking**.

Analogous colours, split complimentary colours, and triadic colours are good fashion combinations.

Complementary colours are any two colours which are placed directly opposite each other in the wheel. Examples are yellow and violet; green and red; orange and blue. Like a yellow gown with a purple sash; also a green dress with red shoes and jewelries.

Split complimentary colours are toned down versions of complimentary colours. In this colour combination, one key colour and the adjacent colours of its complimentary colour gives split complimentary colours. For example, yellow orange, violet and blue are split complimentary colours.

A key colour and its two adjacent colours, that is, colours to its left and right are said to be **analogous colours.** For example: red, red violet and violet.

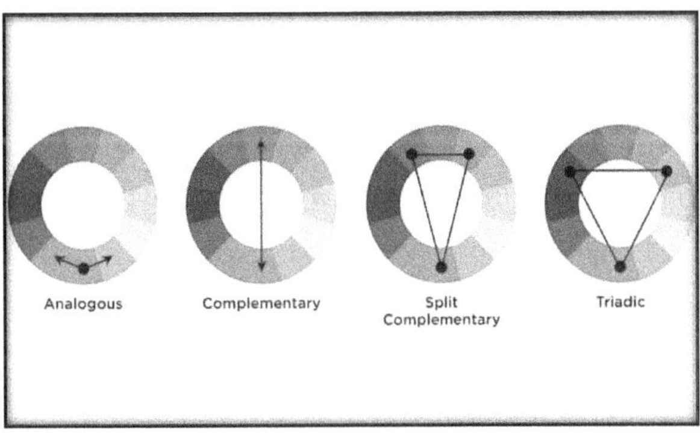

Triadic colours comprise of a colour and the colours after its split complimentary colours. The colours are equally spaced from one another on the wheel. We have red, yellow and blue; red orange, yellow green and blue violet as examples.

I am sure you are wondering where black, brown, pink, peach, coral and the rest colours come in. All colours that are not primary or secondary are tertiary and it is under this category they fall. Red and its complimentary colour, green, would give brown. Some colours are derivatives of other colours. They are referred to as hues/shade/tint of a particular colour. Since this is not a fine-arts book, colour derivations should not be our cruise. In fashion, we are only interested in how to apply colours in harmony. The above defined colour combinations are for colours on the bright side as seen on the wheel. There are neutral colours like beige, ivory, tan, taupe, nude that can be combined to give cool effects. These colours are not shouty, they are plain—the just-there kind of colours. For people who would rather be on the safe and soft side than on the shouty side, these colours might just work for you. Another way to

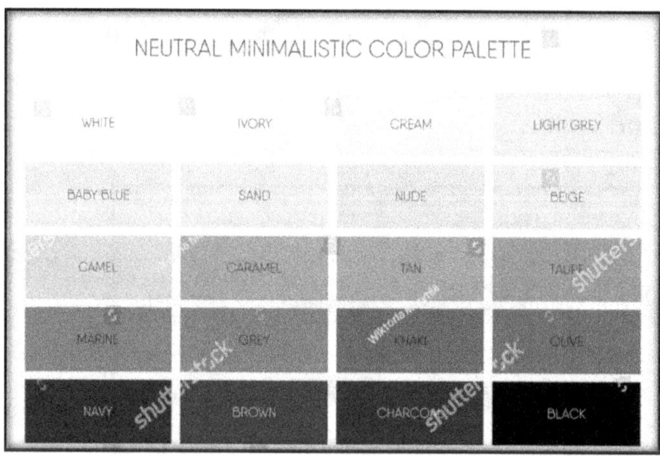

combine colours is by being monochromatic. What this means is wearing different shades of a particular colour, say, violet— your dress can be lilac, with purple belt and foot wear and probably violet jewelries and/or fascinator.

When it comes to colours, you can choose to play around whatever colours you choose; celebrating the variety of colours life offers. Just be sure to differentiate yourself from a circus clown. Enough of the theories, let's have a list of various combinations to try out.

You would stumble on a lot of colour combination options/palette on the net. There's no way I can cover all there is. There are numerous colour shades out there with all sorts of names. I like the indigenous names we've ascribed to some of them like onion purple, pepper red, jollof orange, cockroach brown, grasshopper green, mango yellow and the likes. Remember, these combinations are not limited to the fabrics alone; the colours could involve other fashion accessories.

Fashion to me, is everything from head to toe. You could go something like;

- Red, white and pink
- Red, burgundy and gold
- There's something cool about red, white and grey
- Grey, white, black and red
- Imagine yourself in a white shirt, a turquoise below-the-knee straight skirt, a coral red jacket and turquoise shoes. Uh-la-la. Classy.
- Persian blue (royal blue), white and black
- Red, camel, navy blue and black, and a host of others

Coffee brown can go with ivory, teal, nude, lilac, butter, black, violet, dark orange, red, and so on.

Purple can match caramel, red, violet, nude, coral, lilac, apple green, light and dark brown, and so on.

Orange can be blended with light and dark brown, Persian blue (royal blue), turquoise, cream, khaki, beige, marine blue, black, mint green, yellow, etc.

Coral red can have cyan, ivory, beige, baby blue, light grey, olive, off white, teal, etc as buddies.

Peach works well with colours like maroon, chartreuse green, forest green (Nigerian green), olive green, caramel, sea green, nude, yellow, and so on.

Teal enjoys the company of cream, taupe, brown, mustard yellow, red, orange, sand, sea green, camel, black, etc.

Tan rolls well with lilac, red, orange, burgundy, nude, coffee, navy blue, marine, sand, beige, olive green, forest green, and so on.

Some unpopular two -colour combinations

- Taupe and mustard yellow
- Grey and violet green
- Turquoise and butter
- Coral and purple
- Army green and light grey
- Pear green and orange
- Orange and dark orange
- Ivory and marine blue
- Coral and butter
- Hot pink and fuchsia pink
- Baby pink and tan
- Gold and mint green
- Brown and magenta
- Yellow and turquoise
- Light grey and coral
- Light pink and marine blue
- Orange and khaki green

For the males, some of the colours above aren't just your thing. What business do you have with hot pink and fuchsia pink combo? The neutral minimalistic colour palette as indicated in one of the pictures above should make a major percentage of your wardrobe. Even if a shouty colour is to be used, it should be toned down with these colours. Striking a balance is key. For instance, you could wear a fuchsia pink t-shirt on blue jeans with a taupe jacket and footwear, and a burgundy socks. Cut through a black outfit with light colours like pink, sky blue, white.

Jacket and trouser combos you may want to try are:

GREY JACKET: Black, white and grey trousers.

NAVY JACKET: Grey, white, navy and black trousers.

BLUE JACKET: Beige, grey, white and navy trousers.

BLACK JACKET: White, grey, beige trousers.

BEIGE JACKET: Army green, grey, blue and white trousers.

BROWN JACKET: Beige, brown trousers.

Just before you hit Runway Street, in your being fashionable, you must see to it that you check these boxes;

- ✓ Clean and neat
- ✓ Comfortable (why wear what you have to be conscious about, checking and adjusting here and there, every now and then?)
- ✓ Decent
- ✓ Confident

♣♥♣

<u>The Heart of Fashion</u>

The heart of fashion is the fashion of the heart. The heart of fashion is not in trends but in your personality. Being fashionable begins from the heart- the inward man. There's something about the inside that magnifies the outside. How fashionable is your heart? Marrying personality with style does the fashion trick. Here are some quotes on fashion. You would agree with them, wouldn't you?

"A woman is never 'sexier' than when she is comfortable in her clothes."–**Vera Wang**

[I want to believe sister Vera Wang meant a 'married woman'. No single lady should be concerned with being 'sexy'. Tell me, what is she looking for? I love and included this particular quote because lots of people throw *comfort* to the wind].

"Clothes aren't going to change the world, the woman/man who wears them will." – **Anne Klein**

"Real style is never right or wrong. It's a matter of being yourself on purpose." – **G. Bruce Boyer**

"Fashion is 30% CLOTHING and 70% ATTITUDE."– **Alessandra Tinio**

"To me, clothing is about self expression. There are hints about who you are in what you wear."– **Marc Jacob**

"Elegance is being equally beautiful inside and outside."— **Gabrielle Chanel**

"Fashion you can buy, but style you possess. The key to style is learning who you are which takes years. There's no how-to roadmap to style. It's all about self expression and, above all, attitude."–**Iris Apfel**

These are great thoughts on fashion. It seems they all are saying the same thing but in different ways. Apart from our distinct idiosyncrasies or temperament, there should be that underlying Christ-like character on which all others should be put into perspective.

Some persons are brash in their appearance; they expose sensitive parts of their bodies thinking their worth is in those things they try to display. Hell, no! You are much better than that. For crying out loud, how can what virtually every woman has be another's assessment of her self as being worthy/beautiful in the eyes of any man?! Like seriously???! You really don't need to show you have breasts. You are a woman, you should anyway! Hey, we all do! We don't need to see its size, shape or texture. Puh-leeze! They all serve the same purpose—for foreplay and breastfeeding. It is for the former some ladies act irrationally, exposing what should be hidden. No man's hand is that large enough to have that entire large breast size in one grab! So what's the point, why the fuss for display? Why front the size? Besides, the BIGGER doesn't always spell J-U-I-C-I-E-R! Yes!

> **You don't need to show us you have breasts, you are a woman. You should anyway!**
>
> **Size, shape, texture are God-given and serve the same basic purpose.**

Let me recount an experience (a horrid experience I couldn't have forgotten in a hurry). Three days after my second childbirth, my baby got jaundiced and that earned us a bed at the neonatal ward of the hospital. I wasn't the only one there. I was in the company of other mothers whose babies had been admitted for several issues like preterm birth and the likes. My situation was a bit better, as I had the opportunity to breastfeed my baby hands-on intermittently during his UV light treatment. Other mothers who had their babies incubating had to express their breast milk for it to be given to their babies by the health-care givers. There was this particular woman with very large mammary glands who practically struggled with expressing milk for her baby. Every known food she had taken to help with milk production seemed futile. She wasn't spared of the nurses' jesting too. I felt for her. She expressed so little and had to complement with a milk formula. Perhaps there was an anatomical reason or a medical condition responsible for this, only God can tell. But then Church is life...sorry, I meant such is life.

I feel I am at liberty to sound this blunt and explicit if it will be sufficient to accost the mentality behind the revealing of whatever portion of the breasts there is, as is common amongst women today. Is it for competition, for intimidation, for gratification or what? Is it error or incompetence on the part of the designer/seamstress? What *ex-ac-tly* is the challenge?

God gave us our breast sizes just the way they are. Whatever the size, it is good to go. In fact, with pregnancy comes an increase in its size suitable to handle the feeding of the young. If there was a problem with whatever size, God would have known better to allow Proverbs 5:18-21 (ESV) in His Holy Book.

"Let your fountain be blessed, and rejoice in the wife of your youth,

a lovely deer, a graceful doe. Let her **breasts** fill you at all times with delight; be intoxicated always in her love.

Why should you be intoxicated, my son, with a forbidden woman and embrace the bosom of an adulteress?

For a man's ways are before the eyes of the LORD, and He ponders all his paths."

Beautiful woman, do you know that your feminine structuring and endowments were intentionally designed for the chief purpose of multiplying and replenishing the earth? From the breasts (for feeding of the young), to the hips and curves (to accommodate the birth canal, hence, passage of baby during childbirth). If God intended your mammary glands for public display, perhaps He would have centralized one (as a town crier) just above the designated two to serve that purpose.

A word to breastfeeding mothers: you can still conceal your feeding utensils while at your duty. A flannel or any piece of cloth can come in handy across your shoulder, and over the breast in use, to cover it. You could also wear tops/blouses whose zipper opens from down up behind. In this case, your top serves as the covering over the breast while in use. By all means, don't trigger a conference call! Conference call? Of course! This is what I mean by triggering a conference call. Brother X sees your  innocent, succulent, milk-laden breast performing its anatomical and physiological functions toward your baby, and the image of the breast tugs at or lingers in his mind, if that brother is not a born-again, Spirit-led, Spirit-helped brother, you can be almost certain that that sight of your breast led him to finding another's breast he could utilize to satisfy the urge created by yours. Your action ended up involving two other persons. You started what others finished. That is what a conference call is: a call between more than two people.

In conclusion, if you have a healthy self-esteem of who you are in Christ, you will dress appropriately knowing that you are not defined by your breasts, laps, straightness of legs, 'eightness' of figure, buttocks, hips, size or height. **Christ defines you!** Your real ID is in who you are in Christ. You are more beautiful than what your appearance can portray.

> **Christ in you is worth more than any heady, facial or bodily beauty enhancer there is.**

- ➢ His Eyes, through your eyes, helps you envision a planned, purposeful future—better than any mascara or spectacle there is.
- ➢ His Word/Voice through your mouth is better than any lipstick you can wear.
- ➢ His Headship over you is grander than any hat, cap or fascinator you can put on.
- ➢ His Presence inside of you is more beautiful, more covering, more comforting, more shaping than any clothes you can wear.
- ➢ The Light of His Countenance is more brightening and enhancing than any facial powder.
- ➢ His Steps you walk in make you more surefooted than any shoes you ever have.

You are the apple of His eyes, His beloved bride. He has invested so much for and in you.

♣♥♣

What Is A Godly Dressing?

- A godly dressing starts from the intention. Why do you want to dress the way you want to? If you can strike out attraction (seduction); to feel among (trending), then you just might be set for dressing godly. Are you 'dressing to kill'? Are you dressing to be as sweet as a flower with nectar so that you can attract the 'bees' of the world and find yourself cussing for it? Whatever you are putting on at any point only reveals what was in your heart/mind at the time you chose to dress that way.

- A godly dressing doesn't reveal sensitive parts of the body. The reason for this simple definition is because of the doctrinal differences we have in Christendom. As much as we must be decent in our dressing on the outside, the major show of our rebirth comes from the inside (our character, our thought patterns, our conducts and our conversations). To avoid any form of extremism, there must be a striking balance. Simply put, an ungodly dressing is any piece of clothing that reveals the breast/cleavage (frontally or by the sides) or shows the laps, that is, above the knees like the mini, micro and nano skirts; or bum shorts]) or that is too tight on the bust, hips and buttocks (whether it is skirt or trousers).

> **A godly dressing starts from the intention.**

Answer this: why do people watch porn? Is it to view someone's neck or head or hands or toenails? Is it watched to generate laughter? Apparently, no; it is to view something erotic, something that can excite and elicit sexual feelings that end up being satisfied by either masturbation or the actual sexual act with someone. If this is true, then why have we brought pornography to the open? Why do we have it on our streets, in the mall, in schools, in social gatherings, in advertisements, in the Church? Why have people suddenly turned themselves freely to mobile, unrestricted porn stars without flinching? It beats me. I really don't get it and I hope to never get it. When you dress ungodly, just know you've signed for a porn star!

Handsome brother, you have no business sagging your pants/trousers. It doesn't put you in a good light. You are more honourable than that. Historian sources have it that this uncomely act began within the prison system. Since prisoners were denied belts for fear of using the metal head as a harmful weapon, their oversized trousers easily dropped down to their hips. Some claims have it that sagging was a way the *sagging sagger* showed he was either sexually available to other inmates or he was already taken. Apart from the goofy change in walking steps sagging creates; it is also linked to certain health issues like lower back problems, hip problems and even erectile dysfunction. Hey bro, there isn't any good in this!

The issue of trouser-wearing by a Christian female has been an age-long controversy in the Church. Some argue that when **Deuteronomy 22:5** was written, there were no trousers being worn at the time. From the tunic God made man and woman, this may be their valid point. Perhaps, there was a slight disparity in the general appearance of what was obtainable as the tunic then–differentiating the male's from the female's. Others argue that when man left the garden, he was left to explore, discover and invent things for himself to make his living on earth worth the while; which of course happened and has continued up until today. For everything that exists today, not mentioned in the story of creation like cars, furniture, technology, electricity, buildings, and so on, were made by man (co-creators) through the ability placed in him by God, and existing natural raw materials. If God made everything out of something, man has been enabled to make something out of something!

"And Bezalel and Aholiab, and every gifted artisan in whom the LORD has put wisdom and understanding, to know how to do all manner of work for the service of the sanctuary, shall do according to all that the LORD has commanded."

Exodus 36:1

I know some persons are wondering on which side pants/trousers fall. Godly or ungodly? I am not a trouser-wearing person. But in my opinion, I wouldn't tag trousers as ungodly. In comparison to short skirts, they are more skin-covering, they are preferable for biking, horse-riding, even mountain-climbing and sporting activities. However, I have a **BIG** challenge with the way most are constructed and worn. Most trousers have a way of revealing the shape of the vagina and separating/accentuating the buttocks. If at all one should have them worn, a long top should be worn over them to conceal the dramatic *gluteus maximus*.

> **Man has been enabled to make something out of something.**

Let me ask a question, what will be the eternal fate of those Christian Nigerian Youth Service Corps (a one-year compulsory post-graduate program in Nigeria) members, serving their fatherland, who will be in their khaki trousers when the Rapture takes place? Will they remain on earth for the singular reason that they were on trousers when Jesus came? I wish I could get your answers. This is mine: they wouldn't be left behind because of that. The Kingdom of God is not food and drink, but righteousness, peace and joy in the Holy Ghost. The khaki trouser is a uniform they are mandated to wear for a period of time owing to the nature of trainings they are to receive within that time. The uniform isn't exactly designed for fancy or fit as it were–even though some eventually have theirs trimmed to fit after it has been issued to them. Those ones know exactly what they are looking for.

If trouser as a piece of clothing is sinful, then the khaki should be too. Sin is sin. Sin in the morning should be sin in the night. Sin in Africa should be sin in Europe. Sin in the East should be sin in the West. If trouser-wearing is sinning on a good day, it should be during the service year too. Right? Can it be accounted to the Christian Corps members for unrighteousness?

My submission therefore is, trouser, which is an article of clothing that covers the part of the body between the waist and the ankles, and is divided into a separate part for each leg, is not wrong in itself. There are other clothings, like our underwear, that have the same design and method of wearing. What is wrong is in the how and why it is worn.

So far, we have established that a godly dressing is a decent dressing that stems from a decent heart. Because of our doctrinal disparities, what is godly to one may be 'ungodly' to another. For instance, as a creative, unconventional, out-of-the-ordinary person that I am, I find a one-sleeved garment fashionable. Some may have their reservations about something that eccentric. Others, for fear of exposing their bushy and unkempt armpit, may find such a style offensive. But funny enough, that's a good way to remind one to have that place desert-ified and deforested as regularly possible. Well, as long as indecency doesn't stand in the way of my creativity, I am all out for it. **Decency doesn't negate creativity**. Some denominations frown at exposing the neck, hands and legs. Well, provided faith is in place, it's all okay.

"For whatever is not from faith is sin." Rom. 14:23

- A godly dressing is one that is clean, neat and smells good. It's been said that cleanliness is next to godliness. To me, the worst thing to criticize about a person's dressing is not the cheapness of the fabric, or the poorness of design/embellishments. You can wear a million dollar garment but if it is rumpled, dirty and smelly you've just succeeded in reducing its worth. Let's see this portion of Scriptures you've never understood in this light.

   "Then his father Isaac said to him, "Come near now and kiss me, my son."

   And he came and near and kissed him; and he smelled the smell of his clothing, and blessed him and said:
   "Surely, the smell of my son is like the smell of a field which the Lord has blessed."

   Genesis 27:26-27

If you are familiar with Bible stories, the above verses are from the story of how Jacob succeeded in getting his father's blessings that was meant for his brother Esau, the older one (even though by the exchanged birthright, that was oblivious to their father, Jacob was entitled to that blessing). To deceive Isaac, his wife, Rebekah connived with Jacob, whom she loved better, to get the father's blessing. They had to achieve this by putting on Jacob, Esau's clothing. Such that when he approached his father, he would be perceived as Esau.

Having given the background story, it is clear from the above verses that we all have bodily smell. Everyone has a natural body smell. The smell emanates from those areas with high hair density; like the armpit and hair on the head, the beards and perhaps, the hairy chest. The degree to which a person's smell is offensive is determined by how these areas are catered for. Microorganisms are ubiquitous, and the human body is not an exception. We have natural microbes (microbiota) that inhabit different areas of the body—the armpit inclusive. When you sweat, the sweat is worked upon, that is, broken down by these microbes to produce various chemicals (by-products) that are responsible for the odour that is perceived. That's why bathing is non-negotiable and the use of perfumes/ body cologne is important.

From the passage we read, it is clear that our body smell has a way of being transferred to our clothings. Therefore to wear a particular dress for more than once or twice, having sweated in it is like sending it on killing mission. Be guided please. As much as it lies within your ability, be about with a neat and sweet smelling savor. Wash both yourself and clothes, and perfume regularly. There are quite a number of good and affordable perfumes. Cut down on frivolous spending and add it to your budget by all means. More terrible and deadly is having to cover up a smelly clothing with generous amount of perfume—ah, it makes the matter worse! The mixture is a bomb! See the later part of verse 27 again; whether it was the natural smell or Esau's usual perfumed-smell that Isaac perceived, it was not a repulsive one. Isaac was pleased with it.

No wonder he said, that the smell of his son is like the smell of a field which the Lord has blessed. Smell like the blessed person that you are. Don't scare people away because of the repulsive smell you carry around you. Remember, our body is important too.

- A godly dressing reveals your identity. My senior pastor, Dr. Pastor Paul Enenche shed some light on Exodus chapter two, verses eleven to nineteen. The sermon's topic wasn't exactly on dressing but that insight stuck with me and is very relevant for this point.

"Now it came to pass in those days, when Moses was grown, that he went out to his brethren and looked at their burdens. And he saw an Egyptian beating a Hebrew, one of his brethren.

So he looked this way and that way, and when he saw no one, he killed the Egyptian and hid him in the sand.

And when he went out the second day, behold, two Hebrew men were fighting, and he said to the one who did the wrong, "Why are you striking your companion?"

Then he said, "Who made you a prince and a judge over us? Do you intend to kill me as you killed the Egyptian?" So Moses feared and said, "Surely this thing is known!"

When Pharaoh heard of this matter, he sought to kill Moses. But Moses fled from the face of Pharaoh and dwelt in the land of Midian; and he sat down by a well.

Now the priest of Midian had seven daughters. And they came and drew water, and they filled the troughs to water their father's flock.

Then the shepherds came and drove them away; but Moses stood up and helped them, and watered their flock.

When they came to Reuel their father, he said, "How is it that you have come so soon today?"

And they said, "**An Egyptian** delivered us from the hand of the shepherds, and he also drew enough water for us and watered the flock."

Exodus 2:11-19

When you read the previous chapter and the verses preceding these, you will get the background story. Moses was an Israelite, a Hebrew boy who grew up amongst the Egyptians. He was seen as an Egyptian. The only thing Hebrew about him was the blood flowing through his veins. His accent, his appearance, his clothing, and everything physical, gave him away for an Egyptian. As he fled to a neighbouring country for safety, he was met by some sisters from that region who had left their home to draw water from the community's well. On their return home, they narrated their ordeal with Moses to their father. They identified him as an Egyptian because of how he appeared (verse 19). There was no telling of him having a conversation with them probably exchanging pleasantries or personal details. It only says that Moses stood up and helped them and watered their flock. So it wasn't from his speech but that he looked like an Egyptian.

Likewise, your dressing speaks much about you. You don't need anyone to tell you that a woman wearing a *sari* is *possibly* an Indian. People should refer to you as a Christian from your dressing, at least. That probably should be the first thing that gives you away.

Speaking of identity, 1 Peter 2:9 says that you are a chosen generation, a royal priesthood, a holy nation and a peculiar people. How do royalties dress? They dress with decorum, dignity, calculation and comportment. There's not a trace of haphazardness or randomness. They are deliberate about their looks. They don't appear like they've forgotten themselves or someone forgot them. One can almost hear their clothes, shoes, gait and disposition say, "I am royalty, regard me as royalty, treat me like royalty." Be deliberate about how you look per time. I know I'm on an improvement journey, but one thing you could never catch me wearing was a pair of bathroom slippers; not on my street, talk less of in the market! There are fanciful rubber slippers that can be used since they are market-friendly and water-friendly. Also, there's also no justification to the wearing of hairnet to run nearby or distant errands. If you would need to escape the sweaty inconvenience your hairdo may bring you, using a scarf or shawl should be more appropriate. Don't appear forsaken– God hasn't forsaken you.

You are a holy nation and priesthood; there should be something priestly and righteous about your looks. In those days and even now, especially the orthodox denominations, special garments were worn by the priests. It was that serious and important to God. The garments were made according to the specifications He gave (Exodus 28-29). As a chosen generation, you don't dress like the 'unchosen generation'—the world. I am sure you know how 'world people' dress.

If we will be truthful with ourselves, we will all know when we are dressing right or wrong. If you have a solid relationship with the Father and Son through His Spirit that lives in you, and you have a living conscience and a yielded heart, He will prick your conscience when you don't dress well. As a young teenage Christian, I could almost hear an approving or a disapproving voice in my head each time I looked in the mirror before stepping out. I still do.

The problem most times is refusal to hear or yield to what is heard. It is also the desire to be an Israelite dressed in Egyptian clothes; to blend, conform and gain some level of acceptance with the world. But be reminded that friendship with the world is enmity with God (James 4:4). The problem still is denying the reality that being a Christian forbids one from certain worldly privileges–you can't have your cake and eat it. There's that struggle in some Christians to make themselves feel like they aren't losing much belonging to Jesus. They want to be **'slay queens'** and still be called Christians.

They justify that it really isn't in the dressing as there are stingy, wicked, unfriendly Christians. Sister/ brother, be the well-dressed, generous, friendly and nice Christian! I see a norm some church folks have adopted; adopted so comfortably well that they can appear in the church auditorium that way. They see absolutely nothing wrong. If only they knew how much of a distraction that can be, they wouldn't be so inconsiderate. I was seated in Church one certain day. We were well into the service when a lady walked in, amidst others who attended that service late. She was on pretty high heels coupled with a short gown that was practically begging for its 'latter end to greatly increase'! That was how, by impulse, my eyes followed her— first with bewilderment, then with contempt—to her seat. I was just one amongst the crowd of people who definitely would have noticed her and got distracted too. If you had asked me what the Pastor just said during his sermon, I may not have been able to say a thing because at that point my mind was carried away! This is a fellow sister's narration, what if we hear a brother's side, a weak-conscience brother at that? Somehow, I salute their courage though; there are some who would dress like Mary to Church but like Jezebel outside Church. Christianity is not a piece of clothing we put on and off at will. It is something like your skin you can't rip off. You don't put it on only on Sundays and put it off other days of the week. You don't put it on to Church and put it off to work/school/market.

> **Dressing like Mary to Church and like Jezebel outside Church is also a no-no. Christianity is no piece of clothing to be worn or removed at will.**

Dear Parents/Guardian, instill the right dress sense into your children/wards especially your daughters as early as you can, now when you have the sole rights over her clothing choices. It is part of "training up a child in the way he/she should go."

Teach them to dress properly. Inform them about what constitutes improper dressing and why. Don't think they are too young and have no sensitive parts to show as it were. What you are only telling them is that clothing styles like this are not bad. If they are allowed to wear 'nanoskirt' now, they will see nothing wrong with 'microskirt' later. I appreciate my parents who showed me what proper dressing was, even though at the time when I was young, they were not yet born-again. But they did it from the standpoint of inculcating good morals. I remember a friend of mine who almost placed a bet, to his detriment, that when I gain admission to the university, I was going to add trousers to my wardrobe. I laughed at him. I didn't need my parents to be there or not there to do what honored and pleased them in upholding their admonitions. Not one trouser made it into my collections all through my stay on campus, save for a tracksuit I got when my fellowship organized mountaineering—at least I proved a point to him that it is possible to follow through on one's decisions.

Finally brethren, moderation, propriety and godliness remain the perfect combo. With this you never can go wrong.

"I desire therefore that the men pray everywhere, lifting up holy hands, without wrath and doubting;
in like manner also, that the women adorn themselves in modest apparel, with propriety and moderation, not with braided hair or gold or pearls or costly clothing,
but, which is proper for women professing godliness, with good works."

1Timothy 2:8-10

THE CHRISTIAN AND FASHION

Key Point: A Christian can be as fashionable as her God, as long as the heart and intentions are right.

Food for thought: How does Christianity impact on my fashion?

Prayer

Dear Lord, thank You for the gift of relationship with You. Thank You for Your Grace and for Your Light. Help me to conduct myself as a Christian at all times. Reveal the areas where I still struggle to be in control and help that I hear and heed the Holy Spirit's instructions. Drape me with the beauty of holiness. Impart me with a goodly and godly dress sense. May my beauty be in and out as my outward gives a true reflection of Your dealings within me, in Jesus' Name. Amen.

If you decide for God, living a life of God-worship, it follows that you don't fuss about what's on the table at mealtimes or whether the clothes in your closet are in fashion. There's far more to your life than the food you put in your stomach, more to your outer appearance than the clothes you hang on your body.

MATTHEW 6:25 (MSG)

Five

Fashion of the Spirit-man

It *is no new* revelation that man is trinity. The fact that there is a life after here should help us never lose sight of the fact that man is immortal. Man is beyond the physical. Man has a tripartite nature; he is a triune being. In one of the verses quoted in the previous chapter, it was clearly stated there—spirit, soul and body. When God said "let Us make man in Our image, amongst other things, He meant let Us make spirits. God is Spirit (John 4:24). It also meant let Us make emotional beings that can reason, speak and act—the soul; and to give each one a unique identity, let Us create a distinct look—the body.

The spirit-man is the real you. The body we have talked extensively about to make appear and smell good is just like a building that houses the spirit and soul.

"Then the Lord God formed [that is, created the body of] man from the dust of the ground and breathed into his nostrils the breath of life; and the man became a living being [an individual complete in body and spirit]."

Genesis 2:7 (AMP)

Of everything that God created, man was the only one He took time to form. We were too delicate and important for "let there be" and "let the". He had to mould and infuse His nature (immortality, ingenuity and charity) into us.

As a born-again Christian, your spirit has become empowered again (by God's Spirit that lives in you) to be in charge of your soul and body; to work on them that they transform into and conform to the new you.

It wouldn't be out of place to devote a few pages to this spirit that is this vital. Would it? No, I don't think so.

You may be wondering if spirits wear clothes. Even if there is any such thing, why bother about what people can't see? There's every reason to bother because the spiritual controls the physical. A spirit can exist without a body but there can't be a body without the spirit.

I have read this parable of Jesus a couple of times. I never knew I would be using it here; it makes a lot of meaning.

"Besides, who would patch old clothing with new cloth? For the new patch would shrink and rip away from the old cloth, leaving an even bigger tear than before.

And no one puts new wine into old wineskins. For the old skins would burst from the pressure, spilling the wine and ruining the skins. New wine is stored in new wineskins so that both are preserved."

Matthew 9:16-17 (NLT)

Absolutely! There has to be a match—new wine to new wineskin; old wine to old wineskin. Superb spiritual fashion should match superb physical fashion. The inner fashion should correspond to the outward fashion. You can't score A1 on the outside and F9 on the inside. It is neither comely to have A1 on the inside and F9 on the outside.

There's a way you dress on the inside that transfers to the outward apparel. Haven't you read that virtue left the hem of Jesus' garment? Or even from Apostle Paul's body?

A spirit can exist without the body but no body without the spirit.

"Now God worked unusual miracles by the hands of Paul, so that even handkerchiefs or aprons were brought from his body to the sick, and the diseases left them and the evil spirits went out of them."

Acts 19:11-12

So then, what clothings are we exactly talking about?

♣♥♣

Dress for Beauty and Character

Heaven is one place that was much taught about during my Sunday school days. The things we heard about it were so endearing. The teachers painted the scenery of that wonderful place (that I still dream to see and be) so beautifully well. The Book of Revelation hints us on what to expect and experience there. But it doesn't suffice still. It is a place the human mind cannot fully capture. It is from such a place Jesus came; bringing along with Him, beauty, sweetness and glory. There's a dimension of beauty Jesus brings a person into. It's an aura around you people can't seem to explain. There's something about you they really can't place their fingers on. There was a day I took out the trash to a dumpsite close by. Of course I wasn't looking like I was dressed for a party; just the normal, plain home-look. A young lady (who should probably be in her teens) who was coming in the opposite direction went something like, "Good evening ma. You are beautiful. I like you." I thanked her and went my way. I was wondering if she was someone I knew from somewhere and probably couldn't recognize. But it wasn't the case. I was just seeing her walk that street for the first time. So I smiled and said to myself, "it can only be God." I've had similar experiences a number of times from strangers. No wonder in Romans 13:14, Paul admonished the Church in Rome to *put on* Christ; as if to say etch, engrave Him into your being. Let His Presence exude from you.

"Instead, clothe yourself with the presence of the Lord Jesus Christ. And don't let yourself think about ways to indulge your evil desires."

Romans 13:14 (NLT)

He puts it better in his letter to the Church in Ephesus:

"But you have not so learned Christ,

If indeed you have heard of Him and have been taught by Him, as the truth is in Jesus:
that you put off, concerning your former conduct, the old man which grows corrupt according to the deceitful lusts, and be renewed in the spirit of your mind, and that you put on the new man which was created according to God, in true righteousness and holiness."

Ephesians 4:20-24

The new man is the changed man; the recreated spirit; the empowered spirit.

What does it mean to put on the new man?

- To cut off ties with the old man; to want nothing to do with him again. To treat him like he doesn't exist.

- To learn, know and understand Christ.

You succeed at this by seeing yourself as married to Him; for that is what you are—His Bride. You are not just His Bride, He has called you friend (*John 15:15*). It's been often said that couples who have lived together for so many years begin to look alike or even talk alike. This is possible because they have learnt to blend into each other; they wake up to each other, commune together, and share their lives with one another. God desires communion and friendship with you. He desires to be more than a Flatmate inside of you—a Soulmate! A lot of married couples exist like this. The initial spark in the early years of their relationship dwindles away. There's no heart connection. No

Is God your Flatmate or Soulmate?

conversation. No sharing. No vulnerability. Don't ignore God's Presence, consciously involve Him.

A marital union is a love-based relationship. It is one that should be born out of true friendship. You long to hear your lover's voice; you crave for his/her company; you want to share your thoughts, dreams, and the happenings of your life with that special person.

Now in this case, that special person is Christ through His Spirit living in you. His voice is in His Word—you'll get to know what He loves and what He hates. You'll discover His expectations of you. You will stumble on His provisions for you. He communicates His will and plan for you. You connect with His

grace and loving-kindness (mercy). He hears your voice through your prayers (which is beyond asking for things; letting Him know how you feel about your life's events and about Him). His word will instruct you; it will change the way you think. You will understand what truly matters and conduct yourself appropriately in the same. Any marriage that seeks to be meaningful and endure must be built on trust. In good and bad times, you should learn to trust Him.

One day as I thought about Him in my life and how meaningful His Presence has made my life been, the lyrics of this song just rolled out:

It's boring without You Lord
Your Presence is all there is
Love hanging out with You Lord
No dull moment with You

It's in Your Presence
I lift my hands, not in fear
And I can pour out all of my heart,
and You'll hear
The words that You speak are lamp and
light for my path (my path)

It's in Your Presence
You hold my hand to lead me
And in sweet "koinonia" Your nature
rubs off on me
The treat You give me is exclusive for
royalties (and You've made me one)

Lord I'm satisfied with You
Oh satisfied with You
So satisfied

This song sums it all.

- It means becoming like Him.

"But as many as received Him, to them gave He power to become sons of God, even to them that believe on His name."

John 1:12 (KJV)

After all the time spent together and getting to know each other, a transformation inevitably occurs. Your thoughts become patterned after His; your vocabulary changes. All of these and more happen to the end that there's growth and maturation in Him and the same is extended in dealing with others.

"Till we all come to the unity of the faith and of the knowledge of the Son of God, to a perfect man, to the measure of the stature of the fullness of Christ;

That we should no longer be children, tossed to and fro and carried about with every wind of doctrine, by the trickery of men, in the cunning craftiness of deceitful plotting,

But, speaking the truth in love may grow up in all things into Him who is the head—Christ."

Ephesians 4:13-15

- It means to acknowledge His Headship over you; as a man is the head of his wife. You walk in the Spirit, you live in the Spirit and you are led by the Spirit (*Galatians 5:16-24*). In doing this, you are silencing the old man and his characteristics; crucifying him with his fleshy passions and desire. The spirit-man then takes on new characteristics; which are otherwise called the fruit of the Spirit,—the evidence of His leadership in and interaction with your life—to become the new man. The fruit of the Spirit is love, joy, peace, patience, kindness, goodness, faithfulness, gentleness and self-control.

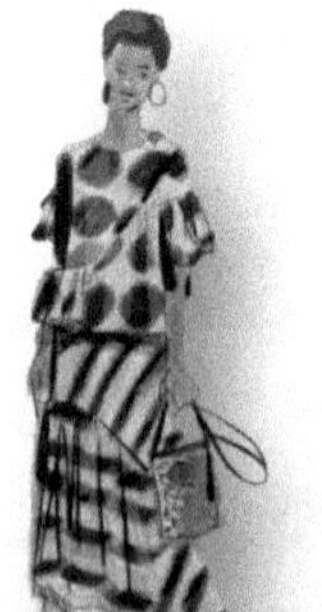

♣♥♣

Dress for Warfare

Another dress of the spirit-man is that for warfare. You see that old man you've just put off? He's not going to back down easily without putting up a fight. He's been married to you all these years; and you think you can issue him a red card just like that? You possibly think he would take the divorce suit you filed against him lightly? N-O!

Sin doesn't like the new you. The world doesn't take a fancy to the new you. Satan also wants to rip apart the new you. They are all at war with the new you.

"Beloved, while I was very diligent to write to you concerning our common salvation, I found it necessary to write to you exhorting you to contend earnestly for the faith which was once delivered to the saints."

Jude 1:3

"Beloved, I urge you as aliens and strangers [in this world] to abstain from the sensual urges [those dishonorable desire] that wage war against the soul.

Keep your behaviour excellent among the [unsaved] Gentiles [conduct yourself honourably, with graciousness and integrity]. So that for whatever reason they may slander you as evildoers, yet by observing your good deeds they may [instead come to] glorify God in the day of visitation [when He looks upon them with mercy].

1 Peter 2:11-12 (AMP)

> **You have all it takes to enforce your victory!**

The good news is this: you have all it takes to win these fights! Jesus knew it was going to happen and so, made provisions for your victory. In fact before the fights came, He had secured your victory. You have everything at your disposal to enforce and establish your already won victory. Hallelujah!

"For **whatever** *is born of God overcomes the world. And this is the victory that has overcome the world— our faith."*

1 John 5:4

Your faith in Christ and in His finished work is so precious; you also need to be everything God wants you to be, and by every means you should stay dressed to keep it.

So then, this is how we get dressed for warfare: **we put on the whole armor of God!** Not some but the whole to stand against the wiles of the devil; principalities and powers; rulers of the darkness of this age; spiritual hosts of wickedness in the heavenly places. From *Ephesians 6:10-18,* they are:

♣ The Belt of Truth:

Wear on your waist the belt of truth. Fasten yourself with truth. God's Word is truth (*John 17:17*). *John 8:44* says the devil is a liar and the father of liars. Also, be a person of integrity and moral courage. To be in the habit of a lying is to create a foothold for him to strike you. Belts are used to hold things in place and in some cases, give fitting to a dress. Keep your life together with truth. Be a sincere person. Let your word be your bond. Be the type of person whose words people can bank on. Let your yes be yes and no be no. Remember that you will need more lies to cover up the initial lie; complicating matters for yourself. Once you are known for falsehood, even your truths will become questionable. Let your words recognize your actions even in the dark— that's someone's definition of integrity!

♣ **The Breastplate of Righteousness:**

The breastplate is an armor that covers the chest against the thrust of the enemy's spear and arrows. You need to be upright in heart; void of offence, evil, hatred, revenge and bitterness. An upright heart is a guarded heart. What flows into your life eventually settles in the heart. The heart acts like the Central Processing Unit of a computer; processing whatever information that comes in and giving out from the same. Proverbs 4:23 says to guard your heart with all diligence, for out of it flows the issues of life. Jesus said that what defiles a man is not what enters into his mouth, for that will pass out through his anus, but what comes out from his heart through his mouth, and his actions. Many a time, the Pharisees and Scribes sought occasions to trap Jesus with his words, but couldn't find any. He escaped their traps a number of times because they could trap him with nothing in Him— no idle words from a vile heart. Jesus' righteousness was impeccable that the devil couldn't lay claims to anything of his in Him (John 14:30)

> **The heart acts like a computer's CPU.**

♣ **Shoes of the Readiness of the Gospel of Peace:**

The Roman soldiers' feet were studded with hobnail boots to give them stability on the battlefield. It steadied them. Be ready to spread the Good News that gives peace. It's amazing to know that evangelism also keeps the devil at bay.

Mathematics had always been my best subject. I wasn't perturbed when it made the list of my 200 level courses in the University; during my study in becoming a microbiologist. I remember putting certain friends of mine through some topics that seemed rather difficult. The more I taught them, the more I personally understood it perfectly. The more you evangelize (talk to others about Jesus, and the peace that surpasses understanding He brings), the more established you are in Him and His peace—unmovable.

Jesus had sent out seventy persons to spread the good news and they returned with great joy at their very successful outing. Then Jesus told them,

"I saw Satan fall like lightning from heaven. Behold, I give you the authority to trample on serpents and scorpions, and over all the power of the enemy, and nothing shall by any means hurt you."

Luke 10:18-19

Evangelism arms you with power. In actual fact, evangelism isn't complete without the demonstration of the Spirit and power. It's beyond preaching. Real, successful outing should be marked with signs and wonders. *Luke 10:17* says, *"the seventy returned with joy, saying, 'Lord, even the demons are subject to Your name.'"*

And this too: *"And He said to them, "Go into all the world and preach the gospel to every creature.*

He who believes and is baptized will be saved; but he who does not believe will be condemned.

And these signs shall follow those who believe: in My name they will cast out demons; they will speak with new tongues; they will take up serpents; and if they drink anything deadly, it will by no means hurt them; they will lay hands on the sick, and they will recover." So then, after the Lord had spoken to them, He was received up into heaven, and sat down at the right hand of God. And they went out and preached everywhere, the Lord working with them and confirming the word through the accompanying signs. Amen."

Mark 16:15-20

Secondly, be peace-loving; be a peacemaker and not an instigator of troubles. Don't fuel strife and make people be at loggerheads with each other. Don't be a separator of friends. Be slow to spread bad news. Advocate for what brings peace. He that sows the wind will reap the whirlwind.

Have an air of serenity around you. Dwelling in peace brings about clear-headedness (you think and strategize clearly), firm-footedness and a corresponding progress.

♣ **The Shield of Faith:**

Shield is meant to protect against the fiery darts and flaming arrows of the enemy. The evil one is set to dish out a lot of lies and suggestions to weaken your resolve and challenge your convictions. You would be faced with trials and temptations, but your trust and confidence in the trueness and ability of God would help you overcome; knowing that He will come through for you. Build strong convictions from God's word, wrap yourself around them; for faith comes by hearing, and hearing by the word of God (Romans 10:17).

When Peter walked on water, in obedience to the command Jesus gave him, to come meet Him up on the water, he simply acted in faith to the word "come" (Matthew 14:22-33). He must have said to himself, "The Master has asked that I come, therefore, I can trust in the fact that He has made it possible for me to come. He has altered the water molecules and caused them to be as hard as ice for me to walk on." Jesus had finalized the possibility of carrying out the command before issuing it. It was on this premise Peter stepped out of the boat in faith. Nothing else mattered at that point but the word that had been spoken and the Jesus he kept his gaze on. The moment he lost focus on Jesus and looked at the storm, he soon forgot the word; fear crept in and he began to sink. To doubt is to drown. To doubt is to lose your shield; exposing yourself to the blows of life and the wicked one. Life is also a battlefield, as you dress up to go out, don't leave behind the shield of faith. Remember, the just shall live by his faith (Hebrews 10:38).

♣ **The Helmet of Salvation:**

Of all the things to wear on the head, salvation was chosen. Yes! To be saved is to recognize the Lordship of Jesus over you. That's why we say, "Jesus, be my **Lord** and Saviour" when saying the sinner's prayer. He becomes our Head, our Master. The One we submit our lives to. The helmet of salvation appears to me like an ultimate protection both in time and for eternity (from the flames of hell). Helmets are used to prevent stones, fists and other weapons that can be aimed at the head in battle. It also reduces the impact of a fall on the head. To hit the head is to affect the entire body. Salvation guarantees your preservation. Christ is your Salvation.

> **Helmet of salvation provides an ultimate protection.**

In the head is situated the brain wherein wisdom operates. Christ is God's wisdom to us (1 Corinthians 1:30)—the Wisdom Satan could not comprehend that led him to crucify Jesus. Had he known, they would not have crucified the Lord of glory (1 Corinthians 2:9). Wisdom is the principal thing (Proverbs 4:7). There are some troubles in life that require wisdom to dissolve; strategy is needed to pull through. Many battles can be avoided by wisdom. Some battles are not even worth fighting; it takes wisdom also to choose one's battles.

"For wisdom is a defense as money is a defense; the excellence of knowledge is that wisdom gives life to those who have it.

Wisdom strengthens the wise more than ten rulers of the city."

Ecclesiastes 7:12, 19

♣ **The Sword of the Spirit:**

The sword of the Spirit is the Word of God. This is an armor that is offensive in nature. The rest are defensive. A wise person said that the best form of defensive is attack. Know when to strike your opponent. We attack with missiles from God's Word. The Bible says in Hebrews 4:12 that the word of God is quick and powerful, sharper than any two-edged sword. The answers to the questions of life are contained in God's Word. There's a word for every situation. Slay those challenges and confrontations with the infallible Word of God. When Jesus was tempted by Satan, He overcame him by countering his words with the Word. Let there be a regular intake of God's Word into your spirit-man. Paul admonished the Colossians in Chapter three verse sixteen to let the word of Christ dwell **richly** in them in all wisdom. Studying of God's word, which is a combination of reading, memorizing and meditating, keeps the word on your fingertips—battle-ready!

♣ **The Sound of Prayer:**

I have seen a couple of war movies in times past. When two opponents are engaged in a sword fight, they always let out a sound or an exclamation from their mouths as they strike their fellow opponent, for example, "he-yah". A battle ground is hardly voiceless. Recall the fight between David and Goliath, there was exchange of words before the actual attack. Prayer is another offensive tool. It consolidates the others.

Prayer is almost not considered as one of the armors listed in Ephesians 6 because it is not external and tangible like the others. It is rather in-built— the tongue (words)! The tongue is powerful. Death and life are in its power (Proverbs 18:21). Depending on how it is used, it is a deadly weapon (James 3:5). Words are like as living things. Of a truth, they are!

Words are like living things.

Watching unto praying (Mark 14:38, 1 Peter 4:7) allows for well-targeted, calculated and specific prayers; like hitting the nail on the head. When David heard what Goliath had to say, he knew exactly what to reply in countering his words. Prayer is declaring the expected outcome. It can be as simple as calling the Name Jesus. It is declaring the will of God hewn out from His Word. It is praying in the Spirit (Ephesians 6:18, Romans 8:26). Engaging in it is an outright show of dependability on God and a call for angelic backup. Prayer is sine qua non.

"The effective, fervent prayer of a righteous man avails much."

James 5:16

Excessive talking, aimless chatter, exaggerative talks have a way of draining virtue out from one. Besides, in the multitude of words, sin is not lacking (Proverbs 10:19). Exaggeration and falsehood are close relatives. Knowing when to be quiet is a plus; it prepares a good prayer ground. It concentrates strength and focus.

"In quietness and confidence shall your strength be."

Isaiah 30:15

Was this the strategy Joshua used when he led the Israelites in a match round the city of Jericho quietly for six days? (Joshua 6: 10-21)

♣♥♣

Dress for Praise

"...the garment of praise for the spirit of heaviness..."

Isaiah 61:3

This particular clothing type is like an undergarment that is worn next to the skin. It is relevant for other garment types. God created us for His praise! He formed us to celebrate Him; to glorify and honour Him with the fruits of our lips.

"This people I have formed for Myself; they shall declare My praise."

Isaiah 43:21

It is good/sweet to know one's praise, but it is better/sweeter when it is sung by another.

God knows His onions but He feels and enjoys it when He hears it. Praise and worship of our God is one thing we will engage in for the rest of eternity. All we are doing here is just rehearsals. Get used to it.

The garment of praise affects the garments of beauty/character and warfare. A function of an undergarment is to keep the outer garment from being soiled by bodily secretions. Another function of an undergarment is to support the beauty of the outer garment by providing shape and fitness to the body. This is how this works: to be a praiser of God is to establish His Presence in your life. God inhabits the praises of His people. He is at home where His praise is (Psalm 22:3). His Presence is prerequisite for His nature and glory in and around your life. His Presence also guarantees victory in the face of life's challenges.

Praise has proven to be a special weapon of attack. 2 Chronicles 20:1-30 gives an interesting account of how God's people took the back seat of the battle vehicle, folded their hands and watched Commando Praise drive through their enemies; utterly destroying them one after the other.

"And when he (King Jehoshaphat) had consulted with the people, he appointed those who should sing to the Lord, and who should praise the beauty of holiness, as they went out before the army and were saying:
"Praise the Lord, for His mercy endures forever."

Now when they began to sing and to praise, the Lord set ambushes against the people of Ammon, Moab and Mount Seir, who had come against Judah; and they were defeated.

For the people of Ammon and Moab stood up against the inhabitants of Mount Seir to utterly kill and destroy them. And when they had made an end of the inhabitants of Seir, they helped to destroy one another.

So when Judah came to a place overlooking the wilderness, they looked toward the multitude; and there were their dead bodies, fallen on the earth. No one had escaped.

When Jehoshaphat and his people came to take away their spoil, they found among them an abundance of valuables on the dead bodies and precious jewelry which they stripped off for themselves, more than they could carry away and they were three days gathering the spoil because there was so much.

2 Chronicles 20:21-25

See what praise did. Praise
- Provoked the Hand of God into action. "They praised…the Lord set ambushes."
- Brought confusion into the camp of the enemy. This happened in two folds;
    i. They were divided against each other.
    ii. Each divided group served as an ambush. They were their own ambushments.

As is common with battles, the ambushed faces the ambusher headlong and it becomes the survival of the fittest.
- Guaranteed absolute victory. "No one escaped."
- Secured gains; it procured profit.

Another account of praise and victory is told of Paul and Silas in Acts 16: 16-38. They prayed and praised and as they did, a customized earthquake occurred in the prison yard; shaking the foundations of the prison. Their praise brought down God's Presence that caused the quaking of the earth.

"The mountains quake before Him, the hills melt, and the earth heaves at His presence. Yes, the world and all who dwell in it."   Nahum 1:5

We were told what happened in the prison yard, we don't know what happened overnight in the rooms of the magistrates who had Paul and Silas thrown into the prison. I am sure God must have given them a stern warning if they loved their lives because verse 35 says that as it became day, the magistrates sent the officers, saying, "Let those men go." They obviously feared for their heads (laughs). It is good to note that the profits their praise procured were the salvation of the souls of the keeper of the prison and his household!

Be a person of praise. Shout to the King. Rejoice in the Lord. Sing psalms and spiritual songs. Saturate your atmosphere with songs of worship. Live to worship; worship to live.
Get your praise on!

FASHION OF THE SPIRIT-MAN

Key Point: A well-dressed spirit-man is a spiritual heavyweight.

Food for thought: On a scale of 1-10, where does the matching of the fashion of my spirit-man and the fashion of my outward man fall? How dressed is my spirit-man?

Prayer

Heavenly Father, marvelous are Your works, and that my soul knows very well. Thank you for Your grace that brought with it, salvation and tutorials on how to say no to ungodliness and worldly lusts. It is on this grace I place demands to escape the corruption of fleshly lust; to partake of your divine nature and enjoy perpetual victory over the enemy and battles of life. I walk in the fullness of all the things You have given me that pertain to life and godliness. Let the beauty of the Lord be seen in me; all His wondrous compassion and purity. Oh Thou Spirit Divine, all my nature refine; till the beauty of the Lord be seen in me. Help me be at my true fashioned best, in Jesus' Name, Amen.

A good reputation is better than a fat bank account. Your
death date tells more than your birth date.
ECCLESIASTES 7:1 (MSG)

I, wisdom, dwell together with prudence; I possess knowledge
and discretion.
PROVERBS 8:12 (NIV)

Six

Dear Christian Fashion Designer

This **book wouldn't be** complete if a space to address Christian Fashion Designers is not created! This chapter would take on a question and answer format. These were questions directed at me during an exclusive interview with Damsel Arise Publications and in their monthly online group forum; and a few extra I came up with. There's no better person to talk to you than a Christian Fashion Designer. I am glad and proud to be one.   We will consider some terminologies before we delve right into the Q&A. Let's go!

♣♥♣
Fashion Terminologies

- **Fashion Designer:** This refers to someone who designs garments **professionally,** that is, has the ability to be original in creating designs. This involves a broad array of skills like drawing/sketching, having an eye for colour and texture, a good knowledge of fabrics (how they move, breathe, drape, react when worn, etc), visualizing or imagining concepts. A fashion designer is involved with every process of bringing his/her creation to life, even models and brand marketing. A fashion designer understudies past, present and future trends which help to design clothes based on customers' needs and likes.

Some persons are naturally gifted for this; as it is with other kind of skills, it can be learnt and developed.

Fashion designing requires some level of passion, expertise, hard work and darnedest patience!

- **Tailor:** This is a person who makes, repairs or alters clothes professionally, especially suits and men's clothing.

  Tailors may form new pieces of clothing from patterns or designs or make changes to existing garments to achieve a proper fit for customers. Tailors can work with a designer to translate designs into finished pieces of clothing.

  A female tailor is called a tailoress.

- **Seamstress:** A woman who sews clothes professionally is a seamstress.

  A seamstress can be likened to a tailor in that she can also make adjustments; however, her main task is to bring those garment pieces together. She can make adjustments, sew seams, hems, add zippers, buttons, etc.

Unlike a tailor, a seamstress does not measure, draft or cut the fabric; she only sews cloth that has been pre-cut to specifications.

- **Pattern maker:** This is a very talented person that skills in creating base patterns for the design of a garment. Not all designers can draft patterns for their designs. Some maximize their time by hiring experts in pattern making to help pattern out their designs.

Often times, these definitions are wrongly interchanged and misused. Someone said that a fashion designer is like a company with many departments, a tailor being one of the departments. Pritesh Pawar puts it this way, using the process of developing a building as an illustration, "if a tailor is a mason, then a fashion designer is an architect."

> **"A fashion designer is like a company with many departments."**

From the above terminologies, I am sure you know which you are. Every of these roles is equally important—forget that we make demeaning jokes out of them in this part of the divide.

♣♥♣

Question Time

Q. What are your standards as a Christian Fashion Designer?

A. My standards is Christ. I made no mistake writing standards and mentioning only one answer– Christ! Christ is all-encompassing. He is creative and so I dish out creativity. He is excellent and so I ensure excellence. He is holy, so my works must speak decency. And by decency, I mean d-e-c-e-n-c-y. What is private stays private.

Q. What are your motivations?

A. As an Igbo woman, what else? Money it is! Alright, I'm just kidding. I can work round the clock, forgetting I haven't eaten my meals, just to get done and see the outcome of a design...bringing imagination to reality. I guess that was what it

was like when God created the heavens and earth, seeing that what He wanted became so. In simple words, passion is a major motivator. The sense of satisfaction and the encomium that follows afterward are others.

Q. Any Scripture for motivation? That motivates you to stay in the lane always?

A. Scriptures that motivate are, *"Seest thou a man diligent in his business? He shall stand before kings; he shall not stand before mean men."*

Proverbs 22:29 (KJV)

"A man's gift makes room for him, and brings him before great men."

Proverbs 18:16

Scripture that helps me stay in the lane is Hebrews 4:13

"And there is no creature hidden from His sight, but all things are naked and open to the eyes of Him to whom we must give account."

Q. What will be your word to a younger Christian tailor please?

A. It's hard to stay aloof in the times we are in because even those who profess Christianity don't help matters with the kind of style they demand of you. You may lose clients; have few likes and followership (if you have an online presence). But always remember that, that everyone does a wrong thing doesn't make it right. There are 7000 others who haven't bowed down to Baal, just in case you feel like a Jezebel-threatened Elijah. You are not alone. Keep doing what is right and trust God for inspiration. I have a brother who is into fashion designing too. One day in his dream, he saw a myriad of designs such as he hadn't thought of in reality. That's a way. For me, before working on a fabric, I get my pen to sketch as I ask the Holy Spirit to direct and help me as to what design to come up with. Other times, He leads me to see another person's design that inspires and births mine. Be open-minded.

Q. What can I do if all my customers want indecent clothings; and I need money to pay my bills?

A. Go to the main bowl of the sports complex of Obafemi Awolowo University, Ile-Ife, Nigeria and pray because it is a serious matter.

Okay, that was a joke. Being a Christian means losing some things and gaining some other in a way the world doesn't understand. The truth is, you may lose some or all of those customers because you need to take a stand and make it known. And you do this by letting them know what you can and can't do, giving reasons why. Convincingly suggest to them a slight alteration to the initial design (as regards necklines and maybe slits); assuring them that they will still look smashingly ravishing with the adjustments. Some would consent as long as the main design is well interpreted and not altered. A garment's design is more than the neckline—a little change there shouldn't hurt. Other parameters determine the beauty of a garment.

On the other hand, accept the work; ensure you get exactly the design with the exception of those sensitive places. The client may express dismay/disapproval upon receipt of the finished work. But then the deed would have been done and you can seize the opportunity to explain your actions.

Having said this, you must be sure to be at your A game. You must be excellent at designing and sewing, your works should have neat finishing, you should be able to take accurate measurements that produce the right fit (with little or no amendment), and you should be prompt in delivery and meeting of deadlines. When a customer knows there's a high level of satisfaction with you, she can damn your inability to follow through on any indecent style.

Be at your A game.

Apart from the job expertise, you must marry talent with character. How potential and existing customers perceive you is very important. First impression really matters. Be friendly, welcoming and accommodating. Be quick to initiate a good rapport with your customers. Be organized. There's a way someone who steps into your outfit, and feels like she's just stepped into the right place, will consent to your **suggestive advice** of making a few alterations to her design. Armed with the right knowledge and speech, you could act as a consultant in addition to the actual work of sewing. Many people aren't aware of what would fit them or not. That they liked a perfectly fitting style on lady A doesn't mean the style would fit them as well. Step in.

Be sure not to be found wanting in being your best at the job and see God bring the right customers your way. *You have your customers;* not everyone is. Every pastor has his congregation. It may seem hard initially, but God might just want to see how much of a God-pleaser, rather than a man-pleaser, you are even if it costs you.

This question is like asking if you should take up a job at a brothel or a tobacco-producing company. That's how I see it. The Christian faith is about believing and trusting. When God sees some ruggedness in us, He makes a way; how and where we never expected. It is *He who gives bread to the eater and seed to the sower.* (**2 Corinthians 9:10**). The Christian faith is all about faith. It starts with faith, continues with faith and ends with faith. *The just shall live by his faith* (**Habakkuk 2:4**)

You know, we mustn't all be on the pulpit to preach. The anointing is not only for pastors. You mustn't be an evangelist or a pastor to preach. In this field of fashion designing and tailoring, you can portray the lifestyle of Christ and win souls. As we can have anointed medical doctors casting out demons in charge of infirmities, we can have anointed fashion designers setting up godly and goodly standards; upholding holiness in dressing, and casting out seductive and nude demons.

When God sees such determination, you will be amazed at the gains you will attract in comparison to the losses you thought you had. Like Shadrach, Meshach and Abednego in the Book of Daniel chapter three. Their lives were at stake but they were ready to give up that life for what was right. Did they die in the end? No! They were rather preserved and promoted. That's how it works almost all the time. Joseph is another case study. His refusal to be lured by Potiphar's wife landed him in prison, but he came out a prime minister. Genesis chapter thirty-nine has the story.

> **We can have anointed fashion designers casting out seductive and nude demons!**

Apart from the preaching angle, you could also think outside the box. If you can source the wherewithal, you could go into ready-to-wear clothes. With this, you call the shots. Display your irresistible, excellent work. This is good enough signpost for what you stand for, and to attract the right customers. Also, since adults are usually the major challenge with indecent clothing styles, you could toe the line of children wears; free-flowing wears (maternity outing wears), and so on. **However 'small' you start, think big to grow big.**

Q. How does one's culture/tribe/tradition influence the way you dress?

A. Some persons may hold the belief that culture affects the way one should dress. Anyway, as long as the culture does not make the word of God of no effect, it is fine. I am aware that some traditions contravene the word of God, even as far back as Bible times.

"...making the word of God of no effect through your tradition which you have handed down. And many such things you do."

Mark 7:13

That is why as new creations we belong entirely to a new lineage. My mentality ever since I was a young teenager has always been that I belong to the Jesus tribe—a 'Zionite', and not to any tribe of this world. **The moment you become a believer, you cease to be tribally/traditionally sentimental.**

If in those days our ladies tied a wrapper around their breasts and waists, exposing a part of their stomach and laps (as we see in Nigerian epic movies), we take it that they operated entirely in ignorance. Don't forget that historically, the only people/country/tribe that had the light of the truth were the Jews/Israelites. All other tribes/people/languages were 'Greeks' having their own gods and creeds. The gospel of Christ comes with light. The light of the gospel we have received does change a lot of things. It illuminates darkness and causes a mental transformation. We can't keep living in the dark past. Living in the past is dwelling in ignorance.

Q. Is it wrong to place high price tags?

A. If you are both a fashion designer and a tailor, you will agree with me that those are pretty tasking roles. There are no fixed prices when it comes to these things. The simplicity or complexity of styles varies. One thing you must bear in mind is that the laborer is worthy of his wages (Luke 10:7)

Consider the following when pricing: the cost of materials and accessories to be used,

The effort and time that will be required in putting the garment together,

The difficulty of fabric workability and,

The intricacies involved with the style in question.

Q. How can one handle fashion trends? (For fashion consumers)

A. I was a spoilt child when it came to fashion; spoilt in a good sense anyway because my mother who equally was a fashion designer set my own trends for me! I didn't know what 'Mary Amaka' (a popular style trending for kids at the time) was. She made my own unique, matured–yet girlish–styles for me. That kind of stuck with me. I would rather let trend pass, before I trend the trend. Doing what everybody does is not exactly my thing. Now that's personal.

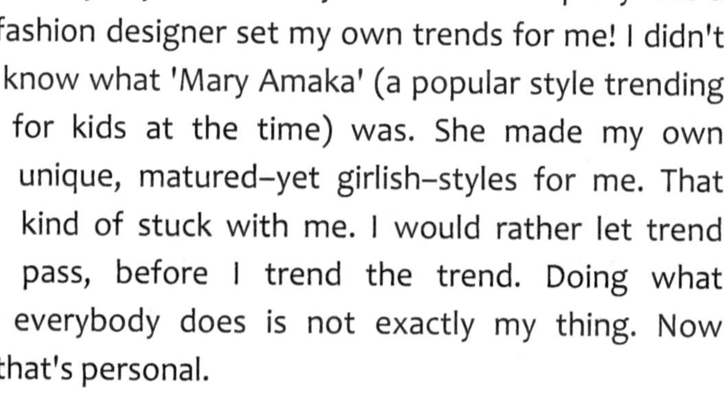

The only constant thing they say is change. Nothing stays the same especially with fashion. Fashion evolves, fashion revolves. To follow trends, you must really be up and ready for it. A fashion trend is a particular style popular at a given point in time; seasons come, seasons go. This means you are changing with every season like a poikilothermic creature. Also, you must bear in mind that some trends come with neck-slicing ability (you know what I mean?)...they are pocket-resizing (laughs). You must be naturally up to par for trends or else compromise may not be far from you to meet up by all means. You are in competition with no one.

Be you, keep it real!

DEAR CHRISTIAN FASHION DESIGNER

Key Point: There's a need to be full of God and well-armed with the right knowledge for excellence and 'ministry' in the fashion industry.

Food for thought: In what ways can I carry God into my fashion business?

Prayer

My Maker, thank You for gifting me with the skill of fashion designing and tailoring. I realize that talents are for purpose, profit and pleasure. I ask that I be my best at what I do and honour You with the works of my hands. I receive grace for ingenuity and creative designs. Anoint me afresh to be a gatekeeper in the spirit realm of fashion. Give me the boldness to speak the truth in love. Bless and prosper the works of my hands. Every client, profit and contract that is mine, I call you forth: come to me, in Jesus' Name. Amen.

Appendix 1

PRAYER OF SALVATION

Being a Christian requires nothing but your 'believing'. It is in believing you receive the power to become a son/daughter/child of God.

"But as many as received Him, to them He gave power to become the sons of God, even to them that believe on His name."

John 1:12 (KJV)

"For God so love the world that He gave His only begotten Son, that whoever believes in Him, should not perish but have everlasting life."

John 3:16

Lord Jesus, I am so sorry. I acknowledge I am a sinner and that I have greatly wronged You. I confess my sins and I forsake them. Cleanse me from all my unrighteousness. I admit my need for You. I believe You died and rose again for the forgiveness of my sins. This day, I ask that You come into my life and begin a new love relationship with me. Deliver me from the power of sin and death. Be my Lord and Savior. Make me a new person and empower me to live all my days for You, in Jesus' name, Amen.
Thank You Lord.

Congratulations! You are a new creation. You are born again! If you said those prayer lines with all your heart, you should feel ease and joy unspeakable!

Like every seed, you need to grow. Find a Bible-believing Church to plant your feet and grow.

I would love to hear from you.

Write me at amiephoebe@gmail.com

Appendix 2

WHY SO MANY SCRIPTURAL VERSES?

One-quarter part of the volume of this book is Scriptural verses from different Bible translations. This deliberate act is to point it out to us again that the Bible has answers for virtually everything that affects the human species. The Bible communicates God's guidelines for a meaningful existence on planet earth. It's been often referred to as the Manufacturer's (God) Manual for the smooth operation of His product—man. Another reason for the generous scriptural usage is to "rightly divide the word of truth."

The use of more than one Bible translation helps to provide clearer, fresher, newer and deeper submissions; from various Bible translators, to verses we have grown so familiar with or had a challenge understanding.

AMP *The Amplified Bible*
Grand Rapids: Zondervan (1965)

ESV *English Standard Version*
Good News publishers (2001)

KJV *King James Version*

MSG *The Message*
Colorado Springs: NavPress (2003)

NKJV *New King James Version*
Nashville: Thomas Nelson Publishers (1982)

NLT   *The New Living Translation*
Wheaton, IL: Tyndale House Publishers (1994, 2004)

~ 142 ~

NLT   *The New Living Translation*
Wheaton, IL: Tyndale House Publishers (1994, 2004)